THE LAST CHAPTER

A Memoir

THE LAST CHAPTER

A Memoir

TONY WHELAN

Matador
5 Weir Road
Kibworth Beauchamp
Leicester LE8 0LQ, UK
Tel: (+44) 116 279 2299
Fax: (+44) 116 279 2277
Email: books@troubador.co.uk
Web: www.troubador.co.uk/matador

ISBN 978 1848 764 958

British Library Cataloguing in Publication Data.
A catalogue record for this book is available from the British Library.

Typeset in 11pt Gaillard BT by Troubador Publishing Ltd, Leicester, UK

Printed in Great Britain by the MPG Books Group, Bodmin and King's Lynn

Matador is an imprint of Troubador Publishing Ltd

In memory of my parents and for Mary

ONE

Every summer during our annual visit to the town we drive out to the cottage where I was born and where I lived until I was four years old. It is half-way along a narrow lane leading down to the flax mill and the big house that belonged to the mill owner. No one has lived there for years. The door and windows are boarded up and the tiny garden that once seemed so vast is covered by weeds and tall grass.

It was built well over a century ago and must have seemed a very small cottage even by the standards of the day. There are just two rooms and, when we lived there, it had no electricity or running water and only an open fire for cooking and heating. Water had to be carried from the pump down at the mill. As for sanitary arrangements, how we coped remains a mystery. Being a very small boy when we left, I have no recollection. Perhaps my sisters who are older than me would remember but I am now loath to ask them.

Naturally it was not possible to have frequent baths or changes of clothes but that was of no great concern to us at the time, or indeed to most of our neighbours who lived in similar conditions, as did millions of people throughout Europe until comparatively recent times. We did not consider ourselves particularly deprived or downtrodden and generally managed to live full and contented lives. And, however poor and inadequate the cottage may appear, it had, and will always have, a tremendous asset. It is situated in what I believe is one of the most beautiful areas in the world. From the front door – indeed, the only door – we could look out on the Mourne Mountains, not a vast range by world standards, but still very impressive and beautiful. And a little further along the road that went past the lane there was a spectacular view of Carlingford Lough with the lighthouse at its entrance and the open sea beyond. There were no monstrous new houses then to spoil the landscape.

My mother was a little girl when she went with her parents and her two brothers to live in the cottage. Before that, they had lived a few miles away in an equally tiny cottage by the shore, which in stormy weather would be lashed by the waves. If there was a really bad storm my grandfather would take the children inland to stay with neighbours. When she was very old we took my mother back to see the remains of her first home, but there were only a few stones left.

There is a studio photograph of my grandparents when they would have been in their fifties. My grandfather is wearing a double-breasted suit of nautical cut and a peaked sailor's cap, his shirt held at the neck by a stud: he has a fine white moustache. My grandmother looks severe in a dark dress with a high collar like one of those pioneering American women in photographs of the Wild West. Apparently she was annoyed that my grandfather did not wear a collar and tie for the photograph, but to me the collarless shirt looks just right. There is a hint of rebellion about it.

When my grandfather took up his post as scutcher the linen industry in the North of Ireland was enjoying its heyday and would continue to flourish for many years. I can recall the unpleasant smell of retting flax. Retting was the first stage in the production of linen and involved soaking the freshly harvested flax in ponds and streams until it rotted. There was another smell associated with flax: that of burnt shoughs. Shoughs – pronounced to rhyme with "boughs" - were the chaff left over after the flax had been scutched and were burnt by poor people as fuel. The smell of burnt shoughs would cling to clothes. Often on Sunday my grandmother or my mother would come home from mass and remark that there was a terrible smell of shoughs from some unfortunate person in the seat in front.

As scutching was a seasonal occupation, my grandfather went to Scotland to work as a fisherman for part of the year. He would send home barrels of salted fish. On his marriage certificate his occupation is shown as sailor. This pleases me enormously as the word has such romantic associations and makes me feel an affinity, however remote and fanciful, with the great writers of the sea: Melville, Dana, Conrad.

My grandfather had a very serious accident in the mill. He lost the sight of one eye when it was struck by chaff blown out from machinery that was not properly protected. As compensation the mill owner offered my grandfather and our family accommodation in the cottage for the rest of his life. This now seems a poor enough bargain but possibly my grandfather thought it was better to ensure that his family would have somewhere secure to live than to risk a legal battle with his employer. The world then was not weighed in favour of the poor and defenceless. Besides we enjoyed good relations with the mill owner and his family and kept in touch with them long after we had left the cottage.

I cannot really remember my grandfather who died when

I was two years old. My mother said he was very fond of me. She thought he was a good man, as did my sisters, and I am inclined to agree.

My grandmother lived on until I was nearing the end of my schooldays. She was a strong, quick-tempered, devout woman, who would have endured with stoicism the life of hardship that was then the lot of the poor, and of poor women in particular. It would have been made bearable by close and warm relationships with neighbours, and there were distractions from the daily grind: fair days, circuses, entertainments in the parish hall, band parades on holy days. Above all, she would have derived great comfort from the ceremonies of the Church. In her middle years she had to cope with terrible tragedies. Later as a widow she had to live with all of us, including my father for whom she never cared, and that could not, I now realise, have been too pleasurable. In her last years she suffered from dementia, wandering about the town and having to be brought home. I know that I did not show her much consideration. I am sure she was always good and kind to me and I wish now I had been good and kind to her.

When she left school at fourteen my mother served her time as a dressmaker. As I was growing up she was often at work on a big pedal-operated Singer sewing machine, making and altering clothes for local women. When the circuses paid their annual visits to the town, girl performers would sometimes call to the house to have their costumes repaired or altered. As the circuses were in town only for a day the work was always required urgently. My mother might complain but she would never let them down. I like to think that, as a consequence, even from that remote and perhaps tawdry corner of the world of entertainment, some stardust would be sprinkled over us.

There was a very strong bond between my mother and her two brothers. Although they died long before we were born, their memory was lovingly preserved by my mother, and my sisters and I would always be aware of their short and tragic lives.

What work Edward and James did when they left school none of us can now remember. For two poor young men at that time and in that place it could not have been anything very rewarding. We have photographs of them, smartly suited, sporting heavy moustaches, and looking years older than they were, maybe dreaming, I like to think, of some golden land. So in their early twenties and a few years into the new century, together with my mother who was never averse to adventure, they joined with the millions of poor, dispossessed and persecuted and sailed to the land where it was believed dreams came true.

My mother went to Loudonville in New York State to work in the household of a Mrs McKinley. Mrs. McKinley must have been a very important person in that town. Letters to my mother were simply addressed to her "c/o Mrs. McKinley, Loudonville". She was very happy there, enjoying the company of other Irish girls and flirting with the young men. She always said she could have lived in America for ever. Indeed, throughout the rest of her life she regarded herself as an honorary American. When I was young I was fascinated by her stories of life in America: she would recall seeing Buffalo Bill's Circus with an appearance of the real Buffalo Bill, early Chaplin films, and that quintessential American event, a centennial celebration – of where I do not remember, Loudonville maybe or Albany. When I came to realise that centennial celebrations happened only every hundred years I would do sums to calculate if I would still be around when that next centennial took place. The best I could envisage was myself as a very old man, bent over, bleary-eyed, with knarled hands, on the edge of the crowd watching the parade go by, the bands, the fire trucks, the police and soldiers, and the marching girls in tiny skirts. And then I would shuffle away, my ambition achieved.

Edward, together with other men from our neighbourhood, made the long journey across America to Butte, Montana, to work in the copper mines. Butte had then a large Irish population. I have often wondered what he could have thought on the long train journey from New York. Some months, perhaps a year later, he wrote to my mother in Loudonville: "I suppose you will soon be taking a trip back again. Tell me when you are going and I might go too. I heard they were going to build a bridge from New York to Ireland. I wish it was built, I would take a walk across". He actually wrote "New York to Liverpool" which is where he sailed from, but it doesn't much matter. He was killed soon afterwards in a mine cave-in. The Butte newspaper report of his death said:

"Mr. Collins, being of a retiring nature, was not very well known, but those who did know him speak of him in the highest terms as a man of exemplary character. He was but twenty-three years of age and had been in camp since July 1906. Deceased was a member in good standing of the local lodge of the Knights of Columbus under whose auspices the funeral was held Tuesday, Rev. Father Galligan officiating".

I must confess I am not entirely comfortable with organisations like the Knights of Columbus but I can understand, without any difficulty whatsoever, why in his circumstances Edward would have wanted to join it. I am also happy to know that they arranged his funeral and I would like to think that those Knights who attended wore their splendid regalia. The kindly Father Galligan tried to get some compensation for my grandparents but without success. I am grateful to him for his efforts.

James went to America four or five years later. He stopped in Albany where our family had relatives. He may not have had his brother's spirit of adventure but in his short life he had great trials to endure. He was beaten up and had all his money stolen, could not get a decent job, and at the same time had to cope with the beginnings of the disease that would finish him off. I can empathise with James. There is a lot about this part of his life that would be echoed uncannily in my own. In October 1912 he wrote home: "Dear Father and Mother, I suppose you wonder I did not write sooner but I could not help it for I had three or four different jobs this last four months. I had not got any steady address. I am working in the parcel room of the Albany News Company. I stop with Aunt Lena at the present time but I can't say for how long for I have quite a distance to walk to work". He finishes: "When you write if you know any news around home of any importance send me some because I work in the heart of the city and there is not one from home or around that I ever see. From your son James. Goodbye". James died in hospital in Albany six months later from tuberculosis. This account of his last days was sent to my grandparents by Father Joseph Dunney of St. Joseph's Church, Albany: "I went to see him shortly before his death and he was bright and cheery, made a good confession and received the Rites of the Church, Holy

Communion and Extreme Unction, with real satisfaction. Then we had a good talk and he said how glad he was to see me". You can knock priests around a lot and some of them deserve it but they can be there when you need them. Thank you, too. Father Dunney for being with my uncle at the end. James is buried in Albany and my sister Jean has visited his grave. I think I'd like to see Edward's grave in Butte some day. I just hope the Knights have been maintaining it properly.

After James' death my mother felt obliged to come home. It would have been hard for her. She brought home with her presents from her friends: a bottle of Scotch whisky, and we still have the bottle empty of the whisky, a wooden drinking cup reported to have been made by Indians, and the *Atlas and Cyclopedia of Ireland*. This is a very large and heavy book and is enscribed "To Anna Dear from Maggie Butler, Cloonashanaugh, Elphin, Roscommon Co., Ireland".

I have the book in front of me. It is bound in red cloth and embossed on the front cover in gold with the figure of Erin with a wolfhound, her fingers touching the strings of a harp, and a scroll with the words "It is new strung and shall be heard". It was published in New York at the turn of the century and was no doubt intended to lift the spirits of the many poor and often despised Irish immigrants. There are two parts: the first part contains maps and photographs of the Irish counties and coats of arms of the leading Irish families and the second part is a history of Ireland by A.M. Sullivan. I loved to look at it as a child but would be frightened to turn a page and find a large portrait of a stern-faced patriot. When I got older I would glow with patriotic pride at Sullivan's artless accounts of the heroic deeds of my countrymen.

"Out stepped from the ranks of Maxwell's regiment, a sergeant of dragoons, Custume by name. 'Are there ten men here who will die with me for Ireland?' A hundred eager voices shouted 'Ay'. 'Then', said he, 'we will save Athlone; the bridge must go down'".

After the excitement of life in America, living in the cottage with her parents must have been pretty dull for my mother. But she was a strong woman and I expect she made the best of it, taking part in whatever social activities were going. At her funeral an old man came up to me and recalled his happy memories of her in those days. She had been a very good looking young woman and I think he had been a rejected suitor.

She met my father at a dance just before the First World War. He was a Belfast man, a painter and decorator, who had come to work in our town. My Mother used to say she did not know what she saw in him but he must have had some charm. Apparently he had a good voice and would sing in local concerts, though he never sang when I knew him. During the war he served in the Royal Navy as a petty officer. How this came about remains a mystery. According to his brother he went over to England to find work and was conscripted. Because of his impeccable republican credentials he was certain that my father would never have volunteered. But I have my doubts. There is an official letter indicating that during the Second World War he reapplied to join up and was rejected on grounds of age. He served on *HMS Champagne*, an armed merchant cruiser which was torpedoed and sunk in September 1917. He was discharged in 1919 with good conduct and was awarded £2-14-9d from the Naval Prize Fund. He was also married in Belfast in that year to my mother.

They lived in Dublin during the events now known as the War of Independence and the Civil War. In the latter my father, of course, took the republican side. On the other hand my mother's sympathies, being herself a Collins, were with Michael Collins and she exchanged angry words with her Republican landlady when the latter rejoiced over the death of Michael Collins. There was an echo of O'Casey about the episode.

When I was in my early teens I remember one of his old comrades from those days coming to the house. They discussed together the matter of army pensions, which the Dublin government was allotting at the time to those who took a substantial part in the armed struggle. My father never got the pension. What he did get was a medal and it came in a little cheap green cardboard box, wrapped up in brown paper with the address written in ink. It was a not very exciting looking medal. He threw it on the table for me to see: I could tell he was not over impressed by it. Perhaps, like me, he thought that after seven hundred years of subjugation, after the massacres, the dispoilations, the murders, the long struggles with only death or exile as a reward, and after you've played your part in the last victorious battle, you deserved something more than a poor-looking bronze medal in a cheap little cardboard box. Whatever else I might say about my father, I think in matters of this nature he was a fair man. He never became starry-eyed. Anyway I have his medal still, in its little green box, and with it are the two medals he was given for his service in the Great War with the head of George the Fifth on them. Uneasy bedfellows they may be, but they are going to stay together during my lifetime.

My father never lived in the cottage: there would hardly have been room for him. And in any case he was not a great favourite with my grandparents. After his stint in Dublin he went back again to England, so where I was conceived I could not hazard a guess. But when I was born in 1928 in the cottage he was certainly not around. What sort of life he had in England I don't know. He lived in Salford and, long after he was dead, when my mother was over in England, my sister and I took her to Salford to see the street he lived in. Even then it was a mean street of shabby little red-brick terraced houses. "Just the sort of place he would live" was my mother's comment.

Of course it is possible that he might have had a nice homely landlady who gave him good meals and changed the sheets regularly. But it is also possible, probable maybe, that his conditions were like those in George Orwell's description of lodging house life in the 1930s in *The Road to Wigan Pier*.

> "My bed was on the right hand corner on the side nearest the door. There was another bed across the front of it…. So that I had to sleep with my legs doubled up….All the windows were kept shut with a red sandbag jammed in the bottom, and in the morning the room stank like a ferret's cage".

I will never know the truth about my father's life in Salford. He never spoke about it, certainly not to me. Just as he never mentioned his experiences in the Great War or his more shadowy work for the republican cause.

During the first five years of my life I saw my father only

once. I would probably have been three at the time. He was staying in Belfast with his relations. I think it was just my mother and I who went to see him. I have no recollection of the journey but we must have taken a bus into Kilkeel and then made the two hour bus journey to Belfast.

I remember being in a large room and my father and his relations are laughing. A little girl of my age is playing with me. This would have been my cousin. When I was a little older and we were living in the town she often came with her mother to stay with us. As she lived in the city she was of course much more knowledgeable than me about matters of popular culture and would have seen films weeks before they came to our little cinema. The hit song of the period was "South of the Border". She knew all the words and could explain that, when it said that the lady in the song was wearing a veil of white, it meant that she had become a nun – possibly because she had grown tired of waiting for her man - though that was never made quite clear. Once when she was with us there was a film at the local cinema that we were both keen to see, but nothing on earth could persuade me to let her accompany me. I dreaded too much the reactions of my friends if they saw me walking up the street with a young and pretty girl. I hope she forgave me. She died when she was quite young.

For the first few years of my life I was brought up in a house of women and no doubt was badly spoilt. Both of my sisters went to school and during the day I was left with my mother and grandmother. There would be carts and lorries in the lane going to and from the mill. Neighbours would call and in the summer my father's relatives from Belfast would visit us. I would go out into the garden with my mother to feed the hens and collect eggs. I was reluctant to go outside on my own because of the goat. It was taller than me and would frighten me when it suddenly appeared around the corner of the house. On special occasions my mother would kill a chicken and I would watch dispassionately as its neck was wrung and it was then plucked and disembowelled.

When she went out into the neighbourhood my mother would often take me with her, first in a push chair and later, when I was older, I would walk clutching her hand. Small though my world was then it was not without interest. Not far away there was a little post office which also sold some basic items of grocery. Like our cottage it has long been closed and boarded up. There is a local belief – apocryphal I would think – that it was paid a visit by Anthony Trollope in his capacity as Clerk to the Post Office Surveyor of Ireland.

Across the road from the post office was a large house called Packolet built for the explorer Francis Rawson Chesney, a local man who had surveyed the Suez Canal in the 1830s; another of his claims to fame is that he walked from Tunbridge Wells to Brighton and back in a day. Many years later I came across a copy of his memoirs in a secondhand bookshop in Stockport but I could not afford the six shillings it cost. That still annoys me.

Nearby also was the blacksmith's forge. The family kept cows and every day we would purchase milk from them in a tin can. They were a Protestant family, not that that meant anything to me at the time. They were really good people, honest and reliable. My mother, devout Catholic that she was, never saw difference in religion as a factor in her dealings with others, either in business or at a personal level. I think she would have liked the fact that a member of the Orange Order helped to carry her coffin on its way to the church. The blacksmith's too has long gone. One of the sons joined the Royal Air Force and when he was home on leave he always called to see us and would bring me a bag of sweets.

The longest journey I would make was to the church, half a mile away. On the way we would pass Mourne Park, the estate of the Earl of Kilmorey, enclosed by a high stone wall that stretched for a quarter of a mile. Needless to say we were not much involved with the Earl, who must have had a busy enough life with many titles to his name including that of Hereditary Abbot of the Exempt Jurisdiction of Newry and Vice-Admiral of the Province of Ulster. What went on behind the wall was, of course, a mystery but the place exuded power and influence. I think I found it a bit frightening.

A group of the Kilmoreys would occasionally visit our local cinema. Obviously they would have the most expensive seats, costing two shillings and ninepence. Unlike such uncultured souls as us in the sixpenny seats who would watch any rubbish they would only come to films of quality such as *Mrs. Miniver*, or *For Whom the Bell Tolls*. And when I saw them in their elevated seats I always felt a little anxious in case the film might not come up to their expectations.

Only once did our paths cross and then briefly. At the beginning of the Second World War, as a boy of eleven, I was involved in the assembly and distribution of gas masks for the local population. This was an incongruous consequence of my membership of the local troop of the Catholic Boy Scouts of Ireland, the scoutmaster of which was also in charge of the town's ARP organisation. We worked in the local council offices. The various bits of the gas masks had to be fitted together, a task that required some practice. I soon became an expert and I loved the work. Then one day two of his lordship's daughters turned up to lend a hand. They were treated like royalty. All the work stopped while the assembly process was explained to them. Fortunately they came for only one day, probably enough for them to claim they had "done their bit": well maybe that is being ungenerous. They were both fine looking young women.

Opposite Mourne Park was Mourne Grange, a preparatory school for boys, said to have been the first of its kind in the country. It was patronised by those prosperous inhabitants of the province who felt they shared a common background with the residents of Cheltenham or Surbiton. It strove hard to emulate its counterparts across the water. The school flag was in the colours of Oriel College, Oxford, where the headmaster had studied and the dormitories were named after famous English public schools, Eton, Harrow, Winchester. The pupils studied for the Common Entrance Examination, played rugby and cricket and put on performances of Gilbert and Sullivan. There was something touching about this outpost of middle-class England in our poor unsophisticated neighbourhood. My mother always spoke highly of the family who ran the school. It survived until 1971.

Sometimes we would encounter a pair of nuns – nuns always travelled in pairs – who would stop and make a fuss of me. They would say. "Aren't you a lovely boy. Are you going to the church with mammy? Don't forget to say a wee prayer for us now". The nuns lived in the convent near the church, which was also a boarding and day school for Catholic young ladies. My eldest sister Rita was then a pupil at the convent and my younger sister Jean would join her later. The nuns were keen on promoting Irish culture, particularly the Irish language. The convent's choir won medals at the local feis. The convent girls played camogie and they, too, put on performances of Gilbert and Sullivan.

The nuns were treated with great reverence by us. Men would lift their caps as they passed. In the church two rows of seats at the front were reserved for them. Because they had consecrated their lives to God we believed they would have a higher place in Heaven than the rest of us. But for all that, on earth there were restrictions on their movements. They could not enter the sanctuary of the church during mass. If an altar boy failed to turn up they could recite the Latin responses and ring the bell during the consecration. But only from outside the sanctuary. A scruffy boy such as myself, his head full of impure thoughts, could move freely around the sanctuary, but not these holy women. They could nowadays, of course, but there are none of them left.

I owe a debt to the nuns. A couple of them ran the parish library which was in a little hall near the church and opened on Sundays for an hour after the last mass. There was no public library in the town then. The parish library had several thousand books, many inevitably, of an uplifting nature such as lives of holy people and the novels of Isabel C. Clarke and Annie M.P. Smithson. But there were also adventure stories by Sapper, John Buchan and Maurice Walsh. Whatever its limitations the parish library nurtured in me a lifelong love of books.

All the nuns have long gone. The convent is now a coeducational grammar school, still Catholic of course. Were I a boy today. I might well have gone there and could have enjoyed the company of those pretty girls, whose photographs in school uniform often appear in the local newspaper.

Our church, a large cruciform building constructed from local granite was opened in 1867, when the Catholic Church in Ireland, now free from its shackles, was raising massive churches and cathedrals that would overshadow the older buildings of the Protestant churches. It does not strike me as a particularly attractive building, though no doubt architectural historians will find something good to say about it. We were proud of it, anyway.

It would always be very quiet inside, although we might hear some old woman murmuring her prayers. There was a smell of polish and candle wax. A light flickered in the big brass lamp suspended from the ceiling in front of the sanctuary. There were three intricately carved marble altars. In the middle of the main altar was the tabernacle and my mother would explain that Jesus was in there and I never had any reason to doubt her. I was fascinated by the life-size stations of the cross, carved from wood and realistically painted, the work of Mayer of Munich. They did a very good job, and I still admire them.

I would not have to go to Mass until I was older but I had already been to one important religious ceremony: my baptism. My grandmother and my godparents would have taken me to the ceremony a few days after I was born. It was very critical to be baptised soon after birth as the Church then considered that babies who died without being baptised went to Limbo, a place located just outside heaven, where they would be happy enough throughout eternity but would never see God. Baptism freed me from original sin and made me a member of the Church. When I died, if I kept the commandments of God and of the Church, I would go to Heaven.

The Church was then enjoying a period of great strength and influence. In our parish there was a parish priest, who lived in a large house in the town, and three curates, who lived in a large house near the church. The church was always overflowing at mass and at devotions in the evening. Of course, in the North the Church as a whole was not as powerful as it was in the South. But it was powerful enough. We too had Magdalen asylums where unmarried young women who became pregnant could be locked away to work in the laundry and be referred to as penitents.

Despite its failings I would grow up, like all of us then, to love the Church and its teachings. Every night for many years we would say the Rosary, each of us in turn taking a decade, and afterwards pray for our relations who had died. My father did not take part in the Rosary but that was because he was a man and therefore not expected to. I learned many prayers by heart, including the very long Thirty Days Prayer which it was believed never failed to get a response. I would make my first confession and receive my first Holy Communion, when I knew that I had within me the Body and Blood of Christ under the appearance of bread and wine. I could talk to Jesus and his mother and the saints whenever I needed to and get great comfort from those talks. And, despite whatever tribulations happened to me, I would continue to believe without any shadow of doubt for a very long time.

The verbal arrangement was that we could stay on in the cottage during my grandfather's lifetime and we were still there two years after his death. He had died in April 1930 aged seventy-two; his funeral expenses came to five pounds, seventeen and sixpence. The mill-owner would not have been so crass as to demand that we leave the cottage immediately. But my mother told us afterwards that hints began to be dropped. The cottage was wanted for another scutcher.

I know very little about the local housing situation at the time. There were probably a few houses available in the town to rent but they were poor houses in poor streets and my mother would not have wanted them. But then another possibility occurred. The council were building a small estate of what were termed labourers' cottages a little way outside the town, and my mother found out that there was a possibility she would be eligible for one. They were two or three bedroom bungalows with electricity, running water and toilets. Whether they had actual bathrooms I do not know but that would not have been a major consideration. The prospect of moving into a brand new house, with no more water to carry up the lane in a bucket several times a day and a lavatory where you could sit down in private and do your business, excited my mother and my sisters and my grandmother. I would have been excited too had I been aware of what was involved. The one person who was not excited was my father, who at the time had been planning to return from England. He told my mother that he would not be happy in a labourer's cottage: he was after all, a tradesman. I think I can see his point. There was a hierarchy among the working class and he needed to maintain his rank in it.

But all was not lost. We had a small sum of money . A few years earlier someone must have persuaded my grandparents to try again for compensation for Edward's death. This time their petition met with success. Mr. Bailey, a kindly official at the mining company, was moved by their plea and arranged for a sum of money to be paid to them. How much I do not know, but it was enough for my grandmother to shower the gentleman with thanks and for him to write back: "I feel that the earnest prayers of a good woman will be heard and if so I am more than repaid for anything I have done on your behalf". Thank you, Mr. Bailey; by your kind deed you have played a part in our destinies.

With some of this money we were able to purchase a small house in a little street in the centre of Kilkeel. It cost £70 and the auctioneer obviously did not value the transaction too highly as he wrote out the receipt in pencil. It was necessary to spend more money to make the house properly habitable and this would use up all the compensation money. Even after the improvements we were still left with a house with one water tap, a dry lavatory outside and electric light in just one room. But we were perfectly happy there. My parents would stay there for the rest of their lives and we children until it was time for us to leave home.

I have discussed with my sisters how we made the move from the cottage into our new home but we could not reach a consensus. My belief is that the coal merchant who delivered our coal moved us in his lorry. I presume he swept it out a bit for the occasion. There was not a great deal to move. The largest items were two beds, a table, a few chairs and a dresser that had been made by a local carpenter. We took the coloured pictures of the Sacred Heart and Saint Anthony and the framed photographs of Edward and James, two brass candlesticks, two models of First World War biplanes said to be made from the brass and lead of bullets; an elegant table oil-lamp, two lots of china dogs, and two very attractive vases decorated with pictures of regency ladies and gentlemen. We also took the *Atlas and Cyclopedia of Ireland*, the empty whiskey bottle and the wooden Indian drinking flask. We did not take the settle bed or the lovely oil lamp that hung from the ceiling.

Of course we had to sell our hens and goat. It was funny about that goat. Somebody miles away up the mountains bought it a couple of weeks before we left and the very next day it turned up in our garden. I don't imagine I betrayed much emotion but my mother and my sisters felt really sorry for it. However it had to go back.

I felt more sorry for our two cats. It was believed then that it was bad luck to take cats with you when you moved. So we just left them behind. In common with most people then we treated cats quite badly. I have retained this image, possibly imagined, of my glancing back as the lorry drove away and seeing the cats sitting in the middle of the lane looking after us.

It was not the end of our relationship with the cottage. After we left another scutcher moved in and water and electricity were laid on. When the mill closed down after the Second World War it was empty for many years. In the 1960s when her children were small, my sister Rita used to rent it during the summer. They loved staying there. My mother would go out to visit them and would say it wasn't such a bad wee place. It wasn't.

For over a hundred years the cottage was the only building in the lane but now new houses are being built just above it which will drastically alter the appearance and atmosphere of the area. The mill house is occupied by an Italian artist and his Irish wife and the mill itself is now a studio. Fortunately the cottage belongs to them and they hope to retain it. Perhaps it will survive.

TWO

For the first few days after moving into our new home I was disconsolate and would sit forlornly on the door step repeating "I want to go home". My sisters would say: "Anthony, you *are* home". They loved being in the town.

My mother had her hands full at the time. She had a builder in to discuss the alterations, a taciturn man, who did nothing to put her mind at ease. Then there was furniture to buy. A little shop at the bottom of the street sold secondhand furniture and I went with her to look around. She bought another bed, a wardrobe, a sofa, some chairs, a big washstand with a marble top, and a sideboard. When we got home we found that the drawers of the sideboard were lined with pages from American comics and these were given to me. It was my first acquantance with Smokey Stover, Dick Tracy and Little Orphan Annie. This cheered me up enormously and gradually I came to terms with my new environment.

Ours was a curious little house on four levels. There was a basement which opened onto a small yard. The previous occupants had used the basement solely for coal and there was a trap-door in the porch down which the sacks of coal would be emptied. My mother had the basement converted into a kitchen with a coal-burning stove for cooking and heating. She used to say that the heat from this stove went up through the whole house. The kitchen was never entirely satisfactory.

Sometimes the floor would get damp but on the whole it served us well. It was my mother's favourite room and she would sit there reading in a well-worn armchair in the evenings, almost till the day she died.

The little yard had a lean-to shed and a dry lavatory that backed onto the one next door. I think we probably put earth or ashes down after a major performance. It was emptied regularly by a young man with a pony and cart: not the most desirable of occupations. Later on we had a flush toilet installed, still outside of course. We used newspaper for many years in the toilet and there were never any serious complaints.

The room on the street level was called the sitting-room and had a little sofa, two armchairs and a sideboard. On the walls were the photographs of Edward and James and later the framed certificate of my First Communion. Here we would entertain visitors but close friends would come down into the kitchen. For a long time the sitting- room was the only room with electric light until eventually my father brought electricity down to the kitchen. Elsewhere we had candlelight. The stairs in the porch led into our main bedroom and stairs from that lead up to an attic bedroom with a skylight. My mother also loved the attic bedroom, and always slept there never bothered by the three flights of stairs.

There were six houses in the street with a shop at one end and at the other end a gospel hall. Catholics lived in three of the houses and Protestants in the other three: we all got on well together. The gospel hall was the most unusual feature of the street. There were two services on Sundays and a Sunday school. The people who attended always dressed smartly. My mother would go to the sitting room window to see the women arriving, always wearing hats and carrying big leatherbound bibles. We could hear the singing and preaching. My mother was very scornful of the preachers, who were drawn from the congregation. She would ask: "What do they know, more than me?". But we agreed they were very good people. Every year they had a Sunday school tea party and when it was over the men would bring out plates of sandwiches and cakes and hand them out along the street. We accepted them without any hesitation. Probably they might have felt sympathy for us as, unlike them, we were not saved and thus facing the awful prospect of eternal damnation. The woman who lived on one side of us was saved but her husband wasn't and this was a source of great worry to her. I used to play with her son who was the same age as me. He was quite a high-spirited young man but later he too was saved and became a preacher. I have a considerable respect for people who belong to these wayward religions.

A boy who lived a couple of doors away became my first friend. Cecil was a year or two older than me, extrovert and ebullient and well-versed in the ways of the world. He was a very tough boy who sometimes worked in a slaughterhouse holding the bullocks while they were being killed: I could not even contemplate doing anything like that. Despite our differing temperaments we remained close companions throughout my boyhood. We walked to school together, shared what few books we had and when I was older enjoyed the same films. I think my mother may have once asked him to keep an eye on me and when necessary he would offer me his protection making sure I got away safely when we were involved in scrapes. After primary school our ways parted but friendships formed in boyhood will linger on. In later life I saw him from time to time and always received a warm, jovial and irreverent greeting, even on that last occasion not long before he died from cancer, still in his prime.

The street had many advantages. On the footpath we could play marbles. I split a thumb nail playing marbles and seventy years later the split is still visible. And round the corner past the gospel hall we played cricket. Well, we called in cricket anyway. We used a piece of wood with a handle nailed onto it and an old tennis ball and everyone took turns to bat or bowl. Boys from other streets would even come to play with us. We played under the high wall of the churchyard belonging to the Church of Ireland. If the ball went over the wall someone had to be assisted up to get it back as we never had more than one ball. Of course there was very little traffic then with horse-drawn traps being more common than cars.

Harmony reigned in the street and for most of the time in the rest of Kilkeel. Others may contest my analysis but I believe the population of the town was two-thirds Protestant and one-third Catholic. There were streets where mostly Protestants lived and others where mostly Catholics lived. In the main street there were Protestant shops on one side and Catholic shops on the other. It is also true to say that most people went to shops owned by those of their own religion. There were exceptions. My mother shopped at a Protestant grocer though there was a Catholic one nearer to hand.

Despite its idyllic setting close to the sea and the mountains the town has a rough, untidy look. It could never be called beautiful. The compilers of guide books have a problem finding something decent to say about it: some just don't bother to mention it. But at the time I was more than happy with what it had to offer.

Our spiritual needs were particularly well catered for. There were two churches for the Presbyterians, one for members of the Church of Ireland, one for the Baptists and several gospel halls. Although the Catholic church was a mile outside the town there was a small chapel near the parish priest's residence where mass was said on weekdays.

To protect us against subversive elements, a large new RUC barracks had recently been opened, manned by a sergeant and three constables. There were several banks, two hotels and a variety of shops selling everything that a normal person could possibly need. And, in common with other Northern Irish towns, there was an Orange Hall and a Freemasons' Lodge. The Orange Order was, and still is, a powerful and influential organisation in the town. Freemasonry had for long been condemned by our church and we regarded the lodge building with suspicion and the names of those we believed to be members were spoken in whispers. I was not aware then that great men like Mozart and Tolstoy were sympathetic to Freemasonry.

There was provision, too. for leisure activities. Like all Irish towns, ours had a generous quota of public houses, dingy and porter smelling and shunned by the respectable. A little cinema showed three films every week. Just outside the town there was a golf course and on our most select street a tennis club, both patronised by our middle-class ladies and gentlemen. For the rest there were football pitches, one for the Catholics to play Gaelic games, the other for the Protestants to play soccer. We had no swimming pool but there was a beach, mostly of pebbles unless you waited until the tide went out. The water was always freezing but on a nice summer's day the beach could be crowded.

Near the beach was the harbour. The town was a very important fishing port and we had a large fleet of fishing boats of all sizes. Small coastal steamers called in, bringing coal and taking away potatoes and granite. Sometimes Dutch boats would call. They were always very tidy and the seamen wore clogs. Once a Dutch boat developed engine trouble and had to stay in the harbour for a long time. The crew became familiar figures about the town. When it was finally repaired the whole town went down to see it depart. After it got out of the harbour a bit it sounded its siren. That was a memorable occasion.

Every month there was a fair day when farmers brought in sheep and cattle to sell. Farmers could be cruel to the animals then. Sheep would be left tied up all day opposite our house without food or drink and, if they had not sold, would be driven home again sometimes for long distances. On fair days the main street was lined with market stalls selling clothes, haberdashery, plants and crockery. The crockery sellers would hold up a big dish of cups and saucers and then give it a toss without breaking anything. A black man would come from time to time to sell tooth powder and would demonstrate it on some gullible country boy to the amusement of the onlookers.

During the summer there were visits from circuses and from fun fairs. The arrival of a circus was exciting. First a number of piebald ponies would gallop up to the main street to be followed by the horse-drawn caravans. There was a bit of a hill at one stage and, when the horses began to stall, this was the cue for some of the local men to rush over and push the caravans from the rear. It gave them a lot of satisfaction. I loved going to the circus. I liked the fun fairs too. I was too scared to go on some of the rides but just walking around watching the different attractions was good fun.

An important event each year was the Orange parade on the Twelfth of July. Our town was sometimes the main venue for the Twelfth celebrations in the area and bands would come there from various parts of the county. We regarded the parades as enjoyable colourful events which we would go and watch.

Whatever our views might be about the beliefs of the Orangemen, we enjoyed the music of the bands and we were familiar from childhood with the tunes they played, such as *The Sash My Father Wore*, *The Protestant Boys* and *Derry's Walls*. Like Louis MacNeice my heart still lifts at the sound of a flute band.

Catholics, too, had bands but not on the same scale. There would be a couple of bands out on St. Patrick's Day and the Fifteenth of August. They would play *Kelly the Boy from Killane* and *The Boys of Wexford*. They were rousing tunes, but the playing was never up to the standard of the best of the Orange bands. The Catholic bands could only parade in the main street but the Orange bands could parade in every street.

For a short period after moving to the town I lived a pleasurable and idle life without a care in the world. It lasted until the summer of my fifth year when I was told I would have to go to school. I tried to put off the evil day for as long as I could. But I eventually gave in and soon after I was five I started school and found it was not so bad. The school was on the outskirts of the town. My mother had gone there herself – in fact she was one of the first pupils. She had a faded sepia photograph of her class with a grim-faced schoolmistress in a long black dress and many children with bare feet. There were still children with bare feet when I went to school.

The school was, of course, Catholic and was also then segregated by sex. I went first of all to what was called the infants school where there were three classes taught by a woman. She was quite strict but not severe. My first class was called junior infants and I sat in the front row. She gave us each a sweet, throwing them to us. I missed mine and she said "you're a bad catch". And ever since I believed I couldn't catch things well. That was a very bad move on her part. I could not fault her greatly and I am sure there are many generations of school children who will remember her with gratitude. One boy who went to school with me later in life wrote a pot-boiler novel about the First World War in which there is a teacher with her name. We had a little band consisting just of tambourines and drums. I played a tambourine, the only time I was ever involved with a musical instrument. One day a woman of some consequence locally was coming to the school and had wanted to hear the band. I was at the dentist that day having a tooth out and had intended to stay at home afterwards, but the teacher sent someone to our house to ask if I could possibly come to the school just for the performance. How could I refuse such a request? I can still remember coming up hanging my jacket in the cloakroom and then entering the classroom to take up my tambourine. The teacher thanked me afterwards and I felt really good about it.

Before I passed on from the infants school I made my first confession and first Holy Communion. It was very hard to know what sins to confess for the first time so most of us settled for stealing or telling lies. There didn't seem to be much else we could confess at our early age, such as worshipping strange gods or coveting our neighbour's wife. First Holy Communion was a very solemn occasion and our teacher taught us how to open our mouths wide and put our tongues out. The Sacred Host could only touch our tongues. It was very wrong for it to touch our teeth.

While my schooldays were continuing smoothly there were developments at home. At Christmas of 1933 my father unexpectedly sent presents to his three children. It was the first and last time he ever did this. My sister Jean got a lovely doll but Rita and I got books. Rita got Blackie's Girls Annual, a beautiful book with wonderful illustrations and stories. I was sent two smaller books more suitable for my age, again with stories and illustrations. I loaned one of them to another boy and of course never got it back. But I still have the other one: it is inscribed on the flyleaf: Anthony Whelan from Daddy, Christmas 1933. Why my father suddenly decided to send these books and where he bought them are mysteries. I find it hard to imagine him in a bookshop looking through the children's books. It would be ungenerous of me to think that it was an attempt to prepare the ground for his return. I know nothing of any negotiations he would have had with my mother. And I was blissfully happy with my ignorance. But soon my world was about to change.

I used to sleep with my mother in the double bed and late

one night we were awakened by a knock on the door. "Who in the name of God is that?" called out my mother. She went slowly down the stairs in her nightdress and opened the door and then I could hear her talking with a man. It was my father, who had crossed over the previous night, visited his relations in Belfast then took the last bus to the town. I had to get out of bed and go up to the attic room with my sisters and my grandmother. I hated the return of my father. He ruined the idyllic life I was enjoying. I remember, when he came home from work in the evening, saying, so that he could hear it: "I wish someone would go out". He would grin but it must have hurt him.

I soon became familiar with his traits. He was very fussy about how we ate at table, telling me off if I did not eat delicately. That annoyed me after being indulged by my mother. But he never really scolded us or hit us whereas my mother would give me a smack if I was getting on her nerves, which was often enough.

My father had a reputation for being a bit of a know-all and I, too, am sometimes accused of having this trait. It could have comic consequences. At the start of the war he got a job on the airfield that was being constructed just outside the town. He came home one day early and very shamefacedly told my mother that he had been sacked as the other men did not want to work with him because he kept telling them how to do their jobs. My mother thought it was a great joke. He did eventually get reinstated.

His hobby was working on old wireless sets. We never had a decent radio in the house until after his death when my mother got a new one. Often he would have his work spread out on the kitchen table in the evening after tea. And then you would hear the screeching as he tried to tune in stations. My mother tolerated all this to a limited extent. He would come home some times with another old radio trying to conceal it and explain it away. Still he did manage to get us to hear the statement of Chamberlain announcing the start of the Second World War. And he was always able to listen to the football results on Saturday evening whilst he checked his pool coupon and to the dreary broadcast commentary on the Gaelic games which we had to endure on Sunday afternoons.

Despite my initial annoyance I got used to being with my father. I never really got to know him of course. We never discussed any deep matters. Maybe all fathers are like that.

Moving into the big school was an important rite of passage. We had been the big boys in the infants school and now we would be the small boys in the big school. There were only two classrooms in the big school and five classes. We moved from room to room depending on the lesson. Our teachers this time were men, and they had canes which they were not shy about using.

The first teacher we had was a local man and hard enough in his way. We did not see a lot of him, as shortly after I moved, he became ill and went into hospital in Belfast. Later on he came back to the little local hospital. We suspected that he had tuberculosis. One afternoon on our way home from school, a few of us, as we were passing the hospital, took it into our heads to go and visit him. We were shown into his room. All we could do was to stand and stare at him as he lay in bed in his pyjamas. We didn't know what to say to him and he didn't know what to say to us. Luckily one of his relations came to visit him and we were able to get away. He never recovered from his illness and died in the summer when we were on holidays. My friend Cecil thought it would be a good idea for a few of us to go to his funeral. The teacher's house was a long way outside the town and, after we had walked a couple of miles, we saw the funeral procession coming. We stood by the roadside and waited. Then Cecil had the brilliant idea that, as the hearse was passing, we should stand to attention and give the scout salute. As the procession got close we could see the headmaster at the front with the chief mourners. He stared at us – five scruffy boys who had come to pay their last respects – but he made no acknowledgement. Our modest tribute went off without a hitch and we fell in at the back of the procession. It was like a scene from a John Ford film.

We had some temporary teachers for a time, none of whom we liked. One of them was keen on music and checked us out to see if we could sing. We each had to sing a few notes. It was humiliating. I was terrible and the rest of the class laughed, in a good natured way. We were all pretty nice to each other. Eventually we got a new teacher. Some remember him as a hard man but my own honest opinion is that he was pretty fair. Free enough with the cane but I have no bad memories of him. He was a soccer player and was said to have played for Belfast Celtic, a Catholic team that had to give up because of sectarian bitterness. At lunch times on our playing field we would always play soccer with a tennis ball and he would join in. I have this memory of him yelling at me to pass the ball.

One of the great advantages of having several classes in one room was that we could take in several lessons at the same time. Thus I managed to get through *Hamlet, Julius Caesar* and *The Merchant of Venice*, while I was quietly coping with arithmetic. It surprises me now to think that we did actually study Shakespeare. *Hamlet* was the play I remember particularly well. It was really torn to pieces. Fortinbrass becoming Fartinbrass and lines like "He is still on my daughter" raised sniggers all around. We had a wonderful time with Shakespeare.

At school I began my love affair with English literature. Despite the fact that ours was a Catholic school we really had no contact whatever with Irish culture. This is not the case now and at Catholic schools children learn the Irish language, perform Irish dances and play Gaelic games.

All our English books were good. The best of them, which I still possess, was Blackie's New Systemic English Reader Sixth book. The text, consisting of extracts from novels and poems, might seem incongruous reading for an Irish Catholic boy but I loved it then and I still love it. It opens with a description of the Oxford and Cambridge Boat race taken from a novel by the Victorian writer, Charles Reade. Incredible as it may seem this is followed by William Cory's *Eton Boating Song*. The contents also include Captain Scott's *Last Message*, *The Lady of Shalott*, and extracts from *Bevis* by Richard Jefferies, Mrs. Gaskell's *Cranford*, and Stevenson's *An Inland Voyage*. My favourite item was Sir Henry Newbold's poem *The School at War*, a wonderful exaltation of Empire and of the glory of dying for it.

> "We heard beyond the desert night
> The murmur of the fields we knew,
> And our swift souls with one delight
> Like homing swallows Northward flew.

We played again the immortal games,
And grappled with the fierce old friends,
And cheered the dead undying names,
And sang the song that never ends."

There were a number of colour plates. The frontispiece is a reproduction of John Singer Sargent's *Carnation, Lily, Lily, Rose*. Inside there are two plates I particularly liked and still do. One is of *The Dream* by Edouard Detaille which depicts an army at sleep, rifles stacked with a dream army, presumably of peace, marching overhead. I thought it was beautiful. The original, an enormous canvas, is now in the Musée D'Orsay and I look at it with amazement whenever I am there. It deserves its place. The other is of a painting by the great Russian artist, Yarochenko, of exiles on a train to Siberia watching from a window as the birds feed on the ground outside.

Outside school I read voraciously. The books I most enjoyed were adventure stories by Henty and Ballantyne and later on those by John Buchan, Sapper and George Goodchild. Occassionally I would come across something with an Irish setting such as *My Sword for Patrick Sarsfield* by Randal M'Donnel or *The Green Cockade* by Mrs. M.T.Pender and I would enjoy these too.

Apart from the parish library books were hard to come by. There were a couple of little circulating libraries in the town which some of us boys used. Books which were considered hot stuff soon became well known and we would pass the word around if anything new turned up. My father kept an eye on what I read to make sure it was suitable for my tender age. Sometimes I had to hide books from him.

My mother, too, was a reader all her life. She liked romantic novels in particular the works of Ruby M. Ayres, Renee Shann, and Denise Robins. But she would try anything. She read *Anna Karenina* and said it was good. I used to send her parcels of secondhand Mills and Boon novels from England. She finished up with a big tea chest full of them as she did not like to give them away. My father read, too. He was a hard man to please. There was nothing in the parish library that particularly appealed to him apart from the lives of patriots and not all of them either. He would read westerns but he preferred books by writers such as A.J. Cronin which might have a bit of real life in them. One thing he would not do was read a book written by a woman.

My other great passion was cinema. My sister Jean took me to see my first film when I was quite a small boy. It was *Treasure Island* with Jackie Cooper and Wallace Beery. I was so excited about going to see a film. I could not imagine what it would be like. I thought of pirates, of ships and men fighting and wondered how could that possibly happen in our little cinema. It was a good choice for a first visit.

My mother also loved the cinema and when I was little she would take me whenever she went. The cinema then was on the outskirts of the town, a shabby little building that concealed a world of magic. We always went quite early and would wait outside until it opened. There were two performances, at six-thirty and nine. We always went to the six-thirty performance and were usually the first people there. Then the projectionist would arrive. He had a little shed outside the cinema where he kept the reels of film and, if the weather was inclement, he would invite us in to shelter. Sometimes, lying on the floor, would be little strips of film which would have been cut off the reel where there had been a fault. When I looked at these there just seemed to be the same picture again and again. The projection room was reached by steps on the outside of the building. "I hope you're giving us a good picture tonight" my mother would say to the projectionist. "I believe it's very good, Mrs. Whelan" he would say. He seemed to me a very important person as he slowly and purposefully climbed up the steps to his little kingdom.

My mother's favourite film was *Maytime* in which were Nelson Eddy and Jeanette Macdonald. But she liked many other films: *San Francisco*, *Waterloo Bridge* and practically anything with Clarke Gable or Spencer Tracy. She did not like films about religion. I am grateful to her for taking me to the cinema. Some boys I knew from wealthier families were not allowed to go to the cinema except on special occasions, because their parents thought that films were a bad influence.

Eventually I was allowed to go to the cinema on my own. By this time we had got a brand new cinema, one that looked like a proper picture palace. At the six-thirty performance the first six rows were reserved for children and seats cost threepence. We would wait outside, listening for any sound that would indicate the opening of the doors. Lots of boys I knew would be there, usually boys who were poorer than me but somehow or other could find enough money to pay for the cinema. Every evening those front rows would be crammed and sometimes the grumpy attendant would try to force two of us into one seat which was agony. When the cinema first opened the attendant had a smart new uniform but over the months and years it became shabbier and shabbier. He always stayed grumpy.

While we waited outside we would talk about films. We did not read film reviews. We did not know about directors but we did know about film stars. We admired John Wayne, Clark Gable, Spenser Tracy, Gary Cooper, Randolph Scott, Joel McCrea, Fred McMurray, Humphrey Bogart, Tyrone Power. We also admired lesser people like Lloyd Nolan and Chester Morris and the stars of cowboy movies, William Boyd, Buck Jones, Ken Maynard, Charles Starret, Dick Foran and comedians like Laurel and Hardy, the Three Stooges and Charlie Chester. And, although I would never confess it to my friends, there were women stars with whom I was in love, in particular, Margaret Sullivan and Larraine Day. It was the golden age of Hollywood and we saw all the outstanding films of the era: *Stagecoach, Beau Geste, Northwest Passage, San Francisco, The Prisoner of Zenda.*

There was another source of pleasure. I had the privilege of living by the sea and during the summer when I was old enough I would go down to the beach every day whatever the weather. On the way I would meet up with friends and we would all go together, talking about the important things that young boys talk about. We tried to learn to swim as quickly as possible and I remember the joy I felt on that wonderful day I found I could swim. Of course, I was never a great swimmer and could only ever do the breast stroke, but I was happy with that. On a sunny day I could float on my back in the water and look up at the blue sky and think that this was absolute bliss. Though I have had no desire to be a sailor I have loved the sea all my life. As a boy I would look with awe at that great expanse of water that extended without a break around the world touching the shores of magic places: Greenland, New Orleans, Rio de Janero, Tierra de Fuego, Rangoon, Vladivostok. The countryside could never impart that feeling of wonder.

When I was about ten one of the priests came to the school and asked if any boys would like to become altar servers. He pointed out what a great privilege it was to serve and that, in olden days, kings and emperors would think that the privilege of serving Mass was more important than the glories that came from their exalted positions. I'm not sure that I entirely believed that but I did volunteer. My mother was overwhelmed with joy when I told her I was going to be an altar boy.

To serve Mass in those days it was necessary to learn by heart the Latin responses. I managed this without any difficulty and today I could still make a good stab of serving at a traditional Mass. We had to supply our own surplice and soutane. Fortunately my mother was able to make mine, even putting a little bit of lace along the bottom of the surplice. She got me a little attache case to carry it to and from the church. I hated that attache case. It was like the cases girls at the convent school carried. One of the curates put us through our paces a couple of times and then one Sunday all eight of us had to serve together. I have got to say that I was the only one who did everything. The others never moved. My mother was proud of me. I was a pretty good altar boy during my years of service. People would tell me that I moved about the altar like a bishop.

It was not that easy being an altar boy. I served for a week every month. Another boy was supposed to serve with me but he soon dropped out. It meant getting up at seven in the morning in order to get to the church to serve eight o'clock Mass. It didn't matter what the weather was like. If you couldn't get there you knew the priest would not be able to say Mass. If it rained and it often did, you got soaked. This did not seem to bother most of the priests. But one rainy morning a priest called Father Corr invited me back to the curate's house while he had his breakfast and offered to drive me home afterwards. I sat down at the table with him and he got me some tea and toast. I watched him cut his toast into little strips and put butter on them neatly and I tried to do the same. I expect it was something he had been taught to do at the seminary in case he had to go and visit members of the upper classes. Ever since then I have cut up my toast before eating it.

Father Corr was thoughtful in other ways. Sometimes when he went to give a talk at the convent in Newcastle he would take me with him and I would spend a couple of hours wandering about the place. Then when I got back to the car a nun would come out with a glass of lemonade and cakes. During all my years as an altar boy Father Corr was the only priest who took the slightest interest in my welfare. I don't ever remember getting a word of thanks from the other priests. I think the kings and emperors would have been thanked.

When I was still at primary school both of my sisters went to London to take up nursing. The house was a quieter and lonelier place when they had gone. There had always been friends of theirs coming round telling stories of their exploits. They had been good to me. When I was small they took me to the beach and on picnics and helped me with my homework and vainly tried to teach me to ride a bicycle. I would help them by listening to them recite the poems they had to learn by heart. The first Christmas they were away they sent me home some presents and I was overcome with joy.

Thinking about it now I expect they were happy enough to go. It must have been a bit cramped for two teenage girls in our little house when six of us had to fit into two bedrooms and there was only a sink to wash at. Rita continued in nursing for some years and Jean eventually became a teacher. We have always kept closely together and they have helped me through difficult times. I could not have had better sisters.

When I was eleven years old the Second World War began. At the time I was not especially interested in politics but I could see there might be exciting times ahead. We were all issued with gas masks. One day men from the Civil Defence organisation came to the school to demonstrate the effects of a gas attack. We had to get into a chamber with a harmless gas, and then the man in charge said that if we liked we could take our masks off. When we did so we had to get out quickly as our eyes began to smart. He thought it was a great joke.

It was announced that, in an effort to help the war effort, there would be allotments in the town and my father decided he would have one, an interesting decision for a man who never had a garden in his life. So he and I set off for the allotment with a newly acquired spade and a graip. In fact what we needed was a pick-axe as the ground had not been cultivated for years, if ever. It was very hard work and, to be fair, in that first year my father did the most of it. I helped him as best I could, but I was only an eleven-year-old and pretty puny. But we did manage to plant a lot of potatoes, carrots, lettuce, scallions and cabbage. When my father was at work I would go down on my own after school to see if anything needed to be done. One of the drawbacks, and I suspect that it is a common drawback, was the man in the next allotment. He was a very keen gardener but, not content with tending his own allotment which was always in pristine condition, he felt it his duty to ensure that the neighbouring allotments were kept up to scratch. I dreaded that he would be there whenever I went to the allotment and he usually was. After two years we gave up the allotment. My father realised there was a lot of work for very little return and he could tell that I had no great interest in it.

We had rationing, of course. Sweet rationing was the greatest hardship as far as I was concerned. Clothes rationing was not too serious a problem as we could never afford to buy many new clothes. Food rationing was my mother's main concern. She had gone to the same grocer's shop for years but now she felt that she was not getting her proper rations, particularly of scarce delicacies like jam. She blamed it on the owner's wife, who she thought was giving the best stuff to the wealthier customers. My mother never liked to think she was being cheated out of her rightful share. Though not officially rationed, cigarettes were very scarce and that created a problem for a heavy smoker like my father. Unfortunately I had to suffer as well as he would ask me to go around all the little shops to enquire if they had any cigarettes. I hated having to do so. It was bad enough going into shops where you were known but it was exceedingly distasteful asking in shops where you never normally went. Surprisingly, on occasions one of these shops would let you have a packet and I would go home feeling pleased with myself and thinking that there were a lot of good people in the world.

In 1940 the first soldiers came, units of the Royal Artillery. Local historians have chronicled in detail our military history during this period and I can only provide boyhood memories. They arrived one morning from Belfast, not in army lorries but in all kinds of civilian vehicles and took over various unused premises about the town for billets. It was more exciting than the arrival of the circus. As they came during the summer holidays I could stay out all day watching their activities.

The officers seemed very snobbish. They spoke with upper class accents and generally behaved like little tyrants. swinging their canes and expecting to be treated subserviently by any ordinary soldier in their vicinity. The ordinary soldiers on the whole were a homely and agreeable lot, very like ourselves, in the main poor and innocent. We got to know a few of them. One who was neither poor nor innocent came often to our house. He had been an undergraduate at Cambridge but he fitted in well with us. He left behind a copy of Waugh's *Vile Bodies* and a book of stories by D.H.Lawrence. My father read *Vile Bodies*. I don't know what he made of it but he told my mother I was not to read it.

When the British soldiers left, the town was quiet for a time. We never knew what happened to them. I sometimes think of that young undergraduate who fitted so easily into our lives. He was really not much older than me and he did not deserve to die an awful death in North Africa or Burma or Italy or France. It would have been nice to know that he got back to his studies in Cambridge.

The American army came in 1942 and stayed with us until D-Day. The Americans took over the buildings vacated by the British and built new ones. They also built an aerodrome outside the town from which Flying Fortresses would depart on distant missions. The Americans were different from the British. They had smart, well-cut uniforms and generally were more flamboyant in their behaviour. They were well supplied with chocolates and cigarettes and were generous with handing them around. They were popular with the young women of the town, and with some who were not so young.

There were black Americans stationed at the aerodrome who would occasionally come into the town. To our shame we referred to them as "niggers". I remember a group walking down the street, nervous smiles on their faces, as they were stared at by us poor white boys who thought we were infinitely superior to them.

What I most appreciated was the influx of popular American culture in the form of those thick glossy magazines: *Life*, *Saturday Evening Post*, *Colliers*, *Esquire*. I liked the stories, the wonderful illustrations and the advertisements for Lucky Strike and Marlborough and American cars. I liked, too, the film magazines filled with the Hollywood gossip and articles on minor actors and actresses who were tipped to be the next Gable or Hepburn, but who would sink without trace.

Not long before D-Day the Americans left: the exhausts of their vehicles had vertical rubber piping attached for the invasion of Europe. I expect that the bodies of some of those congenial young men lie in those vast cemeteries in Normandy.

Life for me was wonderful during the war years. I was only vaguely aware, if at all, of the horrors that were taking place elsewhere in Europe and I didn't dwell on them very much. I had seen films like *The Mortal Storm* with their sanitised versions of genocide and of course I felt sorry for the Jews and other persecuted races but well, to tell the truth, it was all happening a long way off. I was secure and happy even if sweets were sometimes scarce. You could say I had a pretty good war.

In the summer of 1942 I was fourteen and it was time for me to leave primary school. I had really enjoyed the last year there. There wasn't much to do and the teachers treated us with respect.

I can still remember that final day, walking through the school gate with the boys whose company I had shared for nine years and would no more. In times to come I would recall them with more affection than any other group I would encounter throughout my life. But our ways would part now and we would rarely meet each other again. A stayed on in the town but most of us went elsewhere in the world, carrying fond memories of those years when life was untarnished by ingratitude, treachery or failure.

THREE

It was time for a decision to be taken about my future. A few of my classmates had already left a year or two earlier to go to grammar schools and the rest would now be trying to find jobs. I was in an unusual position. Those boys who had gone to grammar schools were wealthier than me. But for my parents it was out of the question that I would simply leave primary school and go out to work. They had both lived hard lives: to scrape a living they had often abased themselves before people who were no better than they were but who had education and wealth. They did not want me to experience a similar fate.

And so it was decided that I would spend the next five years continuing my education. If it was not a totally successful exercise, I wouldn't say it was my parents' fault - and I wouldn't say it was mine, either. I suppose ultimately it worked out all right.

The nearest Catholic grammar schools for boys were in Newry, eighteen miles away. There were two, but only one of them, the Abbey, run by the Christian Brothers, was a possibility for me. Whatever else one might say about the Christian Brothers, they provided an inexpensive if basic education. The fee at the time was one pound a term, rising later to a guinea. Of course my parents would have to buy any books and pay the bus fare. The other school was an expensive boarding and day school. Sometimes when I meet people from the area and I tell them I went to school in Newry they will ask me which school. When I say the Abbey, there will sometimes be a pause and the conversation will be steered in another direction. They understood that I would have once been poor but had overcome that handicap.

I have often thought about my parents going into Newry to speak to the headmaster of the Abbey. I can never remember them going on a journey together. I tried to write about it once but the stuff I wrote seemed false. I think about them going up the steps to the front door of that elegant Georgian building and ringing the bell, my father in his well-worn suit, my mother in her best outfit. It is moving to consider that they did this for me. How were they received? What did they say? They never told me about it. And afterwards did they go for lunch or even for a cup of tea? I doubt it. When they came back they told me I would be going to the Abbey but I would have to sit an entrance examination. I think I was quite pleased that I was going to a grammar school even though I felt some foreboding.

When I went in to do the examination my mother came with me, afraid perhaps I might get lost. The examination consisted of papers in English and Mathematics and was easy enough. One boy at a desk near me, who had a shock of fair hair and a really gormless look, surprised me by the way he cheated mathematics by blatantly looking at other people's answers. I never thought there could be such dishonest people in the world. After we had completed the examination we had to wait for the results. I was told my English was good but I would have to improve at mathematics. But I had passed.

When I met up with my mother I just told her I had passed and she was pleased. There seemed to be no point in worrying her about the mathematics. There was a bit of summer left and while it lasted I banished any thought of the future from my mind. I was always good at doing that.

I am at a disadvantage in writing about my time at the Abbey. Student life there has already been described with great eloquence by Denis Donoghue in his book *Warrenpoint* published in 1991. Donoghue, a distinguished English scholar, attended the Abbey at the same time as me. He shares some of my views about the place but we differ on certain matters, possibly radically.

I have no endearing memories of my grammar school days. Indeed what I recall most vividly is the smell that came from the gasworks as the bus approached Newry in the mornings. On the rare occasions that I catch a whiff from a gasworks now I still get that sinking feeling that I experienced then and which would linger after the bus stopped and I walked up the hill to the school. While it may not have been a great time on the other hand I have no serious grounds for complaint. I received a decent if unsophisticated education and was treated with consideration, occasionally with kindness, by my teachers and with good nature by my fellow students. I could not ask for more than that.

There were few refinements at the Abbey. We did not put on concerts or plays, or have dances, or old boys' associations. We would not have gone on trips abroad, even if there hadn't been a war on. The only outings were to other schools for football matches and, although I had no great interest in football, I often went along with the supporters, as a relief from the routine. Once the school went to a performance of *Macbeth* given by a touring company at the town hall, together with students from the other schools. It was a fiasco. The actor playing Macbeth had to stop the performance and plead with his audience to be quiet. To their credit I believe the boys from our school were not the worst offenders. That was the only extra-curricular activity I can recall. It is not hard to understand why. Most of us were from families with modest incomes and our parents wanted us to pass examinations as a way of moving up in the world. They probably did not think that spending time rehearsing for and then staging a performance of *The Pirates of Penzance* was the best way of achieving this. It was something the Christian Brothers understood as most of them would also have come from humble backgrounds.

The range of subjects offered was limited: Mathematics, History, Geography, English, Latin and Irish. During the first year there were art classes taken by Brother Liston. I do not know what Brother Liston's qualifications were in art. We were simply told to copy pictures in pencil. Unlike most of the other boys I could do this very well. I loved doing it and I still have the sketchbook of my drawings, nearly all of them marked excellent. Also during the first year an elderly brother gave some instruction in woodwork and there must have been a brief contact with chemistry as I distinctly remember being involved with a bunsen burner. But thereafter these subjects vanished from the curriculum.

There were few problems for me during that first year. I was older than most of my fellow students and had already covered some of the material at primary school. I was even awarded a prize for coming first in a test. But it was handed over rather grudgingly by the teacher who remarked unnecessarily that I was older than the other boys.

English was my best subject. It was taught for much of the time by Brother Cotter, a mild-seeming little man who could occasionally become choleric. I liked him, he was always kind to me and very concerned about the long bus journey I had to make every day. He had a high opinion of my work and had me read one of my essays to the class as an example of good writing.

In his book Denis Donoghue is very critical of Brother Cotter. "Brother Cotter taught me English, but not well". It is possible that Brother Cotter was not a great teacher of English but you could hardly expect to get F.R. Leavis for a pound a term. His teaching does not seem to have done Dr. Donoghue too much harm. He went on to become the Henry James Professor of English and American Letters at New York University and the author of several highly acclaimed works of literary criticism.

I coped with mathematics quite well during the first year. It was mostly stuff I had already learned at primary school, but in later years I found the going hard. The world of sines, cosines, and logarithms was one in which I could never feel at ease. I am really sorry I did not make more of mathematics.

There were no problems with geography or history. On the subject of history I again part company with Denis Donoghue who implies there was a strong nationalist slant in the Christian Brothers' approach to Irish history. Yet I have no recollection of ever being taught Irish history at the Abbey. I believe that any knowledge I have of Irish history was picked up in later life. I recall that I was taught British history, French history and in my final year American history. I still have difficulties with the Corn Laws, the differences between the Jacobins and the Girondins and the causes of the American War of Independence.

I was happy, too, learning Latin. One great advantage of a dead language is that it is not necessary to speak it. While I have long forgotten any Latin I ever knew I am eternally grateful for one brief sentence translated by Brother Newell, from which Latin author I do not now remember, as "If things are bad now they will not always be so". Throughout my life I have drawn comfort from that pronouncement.

What I could not cope with was the Irish language. Irish was important at the Abbey. In fact I earnestly believe that, if the Christian Brothers had been told that in future they could teach only one subject, that subject would have been the Irish language. They had their own textbook, the famous *Aids to Irish Composition*.

I don't suppose Irish is any more difficult to learn than any other language but at the Abbey it was not regarded as any other language. It was *the* language. There was a fanaticism involved in the study of Irish. Not being good at Irish was the worse failing I could have had. Everything could be forgiven but not that.

I was seriously handicapped from the start as I knew no Irish whatsoever, whereas practically all my fellow students had been taught the subject at primary school. I could never manage to catch up and my feeble attempts at speaking the language always caused some sniggering in the class.

There was another reason for my aversion to the Irish language. The last remaining people to speak it as an everyday language were poor inhabitants of the Western seaboard and so the literature was entirely concerned with their humble lives. They were, no doubt, nice, worthy people, but I had no desire to enter their little world. I would have been happy to have learned French and to have gained an opening through French literature into a world of great romance and passion, peopled by struggling artists, heartless aristocrats, and beautiful desirable women. It would have been worth learning a language to enter that world.

A more frivolous reason for disliking Irish was that the books we used were so pathetic looking. They had been printed in Dublin on wartime paper that looked like chipboard. Totally different from the wonderful books produced by Blackie and Nelson that we had in primary school. A good example was *An Gradh agus an Ghruaim* by Seosamh MacGrianna. It was a really shoddy-looking little book and my copy was eventually completely overwritten by me with the English translation.

I took a particular dislike to this book. It consisted of short stories set in rural Donegal and, even when I could grasp the meaning in English, it held no interest for me. MacGrianna had a hard life. According to *The Oxford Companion to Irish Literature* he eked out a living by translating English classics into Irish, including works by Sir Walter Scott, for the government publishing house, An Gum. Would anyone really want to read Sir Walter Scott in Irish? When he eventually returned to his native Donegal, he had a mental breakdown and died in Letterkenny mental asylum at the age of 89. MacGrianna may have been a genius – as some people now think – but he helped to make my life miserable. I am sorry, Seosamh, to have to say that. May you rest in peace.

Denis Donoghue was good at Irish. He attended summer

schools in the Gaeltacht where he went round to the houses of the traditional storytellers and transcribed their stories into his copybook. He writes that his supreme achievement was delivering a speech in Irish at the Oireachtas in Dublin. I admire but cannot quite appreciate his enthusiasm.

Despite my bad experience of Irish at school, I did not give up on the subject. Perhaps I have always been a little ashamed at my inability to master the native language of my country. Later in life I enrolled in Irish language classes in Dublin and London but like many such classes they went nowhere. One of these days I may try again.

Next to the Irish language the most important subject at the Abbey was Gaelic football. Gaelic football was the preserve of Brother Newell, a little man with a strange unforgettable face, whose expression of pleasure never went beyond a grim sardonic smile. He thought it was very important to play Gaelic football and equally important that the school had a winning team. His enthusiasm for Gaelic football was legendary across the country. We even had a school football song with the same air as *McNamara's Band* which we would have to sing during matches with other schools. It was very embarrassing.

On my first Wednesday at the Abbey, Brother Newell took the class down to the playing fields. He had a simple selection process. He lined us all up and made us race to the opposite side of the playing field. I was among the last. Needless to say I was not selected to play football and, together with the other slowcoaches, was sent off to do p.t.

For a Christian Brothers' school, our p.t instructor was a strange choice. He was English, a former British army sergeant who looked and acted the part. We had a gym with the usual apparatus that gyms have. Maybe it was because I was the oldest I was chosen to demonstrate the use of the parallel bars which I did very well and as a result for the first and last time I was applauded for my athletic prowess. But it was all downhill from then on. Denis Donoghue had the same problem. Like him I was unable to climb up the ropes.

We were pretty religious at the Abbey. Nobody talked dirty or passed around dirty books. On the whole we were of the opinion that women were towers of ivory, or ought to be. Once between classes I made some harmless and, I thought, witty statement about a harlot and the boy in front turned round and slapped my face: that is how religious we were.

At the beginning of my first year we had a retreat conducted by priests from the Redemptorist Order. Redemptorists had a reputation for being great preachers. They gave missions all over Ireland. When they gave a mission in our parish at home the church would be packed. People came from other parishes to hear the preaching.

Redemptorists were particularly keen on battling with the sins of the flesh. During a mission one evening service would be devoted to the subject. There were separate evenings for men and women and my sisters would tell me what was said on the women's evening. One thing I remember was that it was an occasion of sin to be in a room on your own with a member of the opposite sex unless it was a close relative. There were no venial sins of the flesh, only mortal sins, that is sins deserving eternal damnation. Forget about love, about human frailty, if you succumbed you had better get to confession without delay and make sure you don't get run over by a bus on the way.

The Redemptorists were very plausible. They knew their stuff. They did not shout at you. They could take you into their confidence. They made you feel they were on your side. With us first year boys they had a receptive congregation. By the time they had got through their sermon on the sixth commandment any boy still having doubts about the dreadful consequences of what were euphemistically called impure acts, would have been very stupid indeed. Afterwards there were queues of nervous boys waiting to be confessed. Of course, in confession they would be very nice to you and maybe only give you the rosary for penance. But they would also give you a sense of guilt that would remain with you all your life.

On the whole the retreat, apart from the little matter of sins of impurity, was enjoyable enough. We had to observe silence and when we were not at a service we were supposed to read pious works. The most popular were the little pamphlets published by the Catholic Truth Society. The majority of these contained lives of saints or advice on achieving holiness but there was also fiction with a religious theme, sometimes written by a decent writer in need of a few shillings. This is what we tended to read.

On the bus journey to and from Newry we passed through very beautiful scenery but I appreciated the scenery only on the way home in the evenings. In the mornings it was usually necessary to do some revision and also to worry about the lessons of that day.

The bus would start off in Kilkeel with only a few people on board but it would pick up more students along the way and would be full when it reached Newry. Apart from those going to the Abbey there were girls going to the convent schools in Newry who wore dark gym slips with black stockings. There were also boys and girls going to the coeducational protestant grammar school. A few girls from our town went there. They wore attractive brown uniforms and in the summer would have bare legs with ankle socks. They always looked so neat and well groomed. We would briefly acknowledge one another at the bus station but there was an unbridgeable gulf between us. In a way I envied these girls. They did not have Redemptorist priests putting the fear of God into them, nor would they have hang-ups about impure thoughts or acts.

At school the attitude to the war was different from what I experienced at home. One of my class mates had a German mother, a blonde boy who wore shorts, and would have looked at home in the Hitler Youth Movement. His sentiments were firmly with the Fatherland and they were shared by others in the class. At the time there were rumours, not without foundation, of a possible invasion by British and American forces of southern Ireland. Boys who came from the South told us tales of preparations to resist this invasion, of rifles and machine guns being issued to local volunteers. They had such unrealistic views of the strength of the Irish defence forces. They spoke of the one squadron of antiquated fighter planes taking on the Royal Air Force and winning, of the outstanding leadership qualities of their Generals McKenna and Costello, the latter apparently a graduate of Westpoint. It was difficult not to feel some sympathy with the views of these boys. Southern Ireland was a small poor country with only one city of any size that could have been easily destroyed in a bombing raid with catastrophic consequences. But I had also seen the newsreels and I knew that the Nazis were not nice people. When I went home in the evening I entered another world. There would be American soldiers working in the garage across the road from us who would wink at me. They had left behind their homes and families to fight to free the enslaved peoples of Europe. I could not argue against that. Of course I realise now that Southern Ireland was not entirely neutral but liaised closely with Britain during the latter part of the war. I am happy about that.

At the end of the second year at the Abbey I passed the Junior Leaving Certificate examination with reasonable success. I even passed in the Irish paper. I wanted to leave then and get a job but my parents would not hear of it. They insisted I must continue for another two years until I had obtained my Senior Leaving Certificate. For that I owe them a debt of gratitude.

In November of that year my grandmother died. She was in her eighties and had been suffering from dementia, which made life difficult for us but particularly for my mother. Then towards the end she had a number of strokes. My sister Rita was at home during this period and helped with the nursing. I, of course, had little involvement in it all.

One day after school as I was walking up our street a neighbour came out and told me that my grandmother had died. The blind was partially drawn on the downstairs window of our house. When I went in my mother, already wearing black, had been crying. She told me I could go up to the bedroom where my grandmother had been laid out.

It did not bother me much going up, even though I had never seen a dead person. It was very quiet in the room. My grandmother looked noble and at peace in death. I did what I was expected to do, knelt down and said a prayer. Then I put out my hand and touched her hands that were joined together holding her rosary. For the rest of the evening friends and neighbours would call and offer their sympathy. The women would go up to the bedroom and say a prayer. The men tended to sit downstairs and talk. The sitting room was full of people that evening and there were more downstairs in the kitchen. We had bought sherry and whisky and a cake for the occasion.

My mother was too grief-stricken to go to the funeral. I walked with my father behind the hearse the mile or so to the church. As we passed people would draw their blinds. I did not have to carry the coffin into the church. That was left to my father and some of my grandmother's relations. After the service my father went up to the altar rail and stood with the priest while the offerings were handed in. Each person said his or her name as the offering was placed onto the plate and my father then went into the sacristy with the priest to count the money. When they came out the priest announced that total amount. People who could not get to a funeral would want to know the amount of the offering. I noted my father's actions carefully as I knew that one day the task would fall to me, and that day would come soon enough.

The coffin was then carried down to the grave and my grandmother was laid to rest beside my grandfather. I expect that he and James and Edward would have warmly welcomed her. Difficult though she was towards the end we would all miss her.

In that final year of the war I was preparing for the Leaving Certificate examination. Despite all the extra study that year was quite agreeable. We were treated pretty much as adults and given extra tuition where it was felt to be needed. The examination came and, like all examinations was never quite as bad as it might have been. Then it was all over. There were no celebrations. We just said goodbye and then caught the bus home.

I am grateful to the Christian Brothers. These were a strange bunch. Founded in Ireland over two hundred years ago to provide education for poor boys, they have schools all over the world. They enabled people like me to get a secondary education when other avenues were closed. Unfortunately they acquired an unenviable reputation for harshness, even cruelty. I have met men who told me of the brutal treatment received from the Christian Brothers and I have no option but to believe them. Recently the Order has issued public statements apologising for the behaviour of its members in the past.

During my time at the Abbey I never witnessed any of the brothers behaving badly. They may have been firm but they were also kind. I remember all of those who taught me, if not with warmth, at least with some affection.

Of Brother Cotter I have the kindliest memories. Brother Liston, who had made a stab at teaching us art was a remote figure, always polite. Brother Newell had a ferocious reputation and he scared me at first, but I came to realise that he was a fair and considerate person. During the last year, when he would have us in on Saturday mornings for extra tuition, he always provided lemonade and cakes: even then he never seemed very cheerful. The headmaster, Brother Nagle, had an air of world weariness: he had survived a long time and had heard all the excuses. He could be witty. But it was a theological pronouncement of his that I will always remember. One day during religious instruction he told us that he did not believe that anyone went to Hell.

We had lay teachers too. Unmemorable men mostly. Apart from one I thought had a cruel streak. There is nothing more I need to say about them.

After I finished there I did not keep in touch with the Abbey and, apart from those boys who travelled from Kilkeel with me, I had no further contact with my fellow students. The school itself is still thriving. It has moved to new premises further up the hill. There are no Christian Brothers there now, though it is still owned by the Order. A plaque on the wall of the old building pays tribute to the Brothers' contribution to education. Occasionally if I am in the area I see some of the present day students. They now wear a uniform and, according to reports in the local papers, go on trips to the continent and hold dances where they are accompanied by young ladies in revealing evening dresses. I wonder if the Redemptionists still give retreats there.

When I left school I was a shy, skinny, introverted young man more interested in books and films than the company of others. But I did make an effort. I went to ceilis in the parish hall and occasionally I would be pushed into getting up and taking part but I always felt I was too ungainly to dance well. Still, those jolly girls were very tempting and I liked the feel of their soft bodies when I had my arms around their waists. I used to wish I was one of those extrovert boys who could just grab a girl and pull her onto the dance floor.

I whiled away the summer going to the beach and, when I could afford it, to the cinema, with no idea of what lay ahead of me. On the day when the results were due out a couple of my fellow students called to say they were going to ring up the school and I went along with them to the phone box. I had never spoken on the telephone before. The other boys got their results first and passed the phone to me. Brother Liston was on the other end. He read out my grades in each subject and then said "Result, pass. Congratulations, Mr. Whelan". I still remember that he called me "Mr. Whelan". I was not a schoolboy any more.

My parents were overjoyed. It seemed to them wonderful that their son should have passed the Leaving Certificate examination. One local boy from a well-off family who went to the more prestigious school, had failed and they got additional satisfaction from that.

So for a while I went about trailing clouds of glory with people congratulating me on my success. And it was a pretty good result after just four years of study, good enough anyway. The problem now was what to do with my certificate. My parents were determined that I should be able to follow some respectable career. They saw me going to work in a smart suit, owning a decent house and maybe a car, holding my own with the doctor and the bank manager and the parish priest.

There was no one to offer them professional advice. They could only speak with friends and neighbours who knew as little about further education as they did. But they had sense enough to know that the prestigious professions like medicine and the law were out of the question for poor people like us. Even to be a humble bank clerk it was necessary to pass an examination and to have a substantial sum of money invested. The only possibility was teaching. If I had done extremely well in my Leaving Certificate examination I might have got a scholarship to a teachers' training college. But my results were far below the standard required for a scholarship.

Then someone must have told them that, if I went to university and obtained a degree, I could then automatically go on to the training college. They decided that was the route I should follow. I don't remember ever being consulted about the matter. But then what alternative could I have proposed? Nothing else would have been open to me. Maybe I thought going to university would be an agreeable experience.

There was only one university possible: Queen's University in Belfast. I had relations there who could give me cheap accommodation. For a family from our background it was highly unusual at the time to send a son or daughter to university. Young people from the town did go but they were from families with some money. My parents made a big sacrifice to send me to university and I wished it had turned out better. Of course I am not proud of my time at university but now, after taking all the circumstances into account, I am not sure that I could have done any better.

It was settled that I would stay with a relative by marriage, a single woman who lived with her aged father just off the Falls Road. The arrangement was that my mother would send me a pound each week, and I would hand over fifteen shillings for board and lodgings, keeping five shillings for myself. I would also send my washing home each week and my mother would post it back. It was hard for my parents to part with a pound every week and there was also the tuition fee to pay which came to twenty-two pounds a year. I feel bad even now when I think about it.

There was no one else from the Abbey going to Queen's University. Some of my fellow students were going to

University College, Dublin. Queen's was a little frowned on in Catholic circles at the time. It was considered, with some justification, a Protestant Unionist establishment. UCD on the other hand was Catholic and Irish. Of course within a short time Queen's would change radically. In the sixties it was reputed to be a hot-bed of republicanism. Bernadette Devlin was a student there and it was where the Civil Rights movement began. Seamus Heaney, great poet and Nobel Laureate, who could articulate the feelings of Northern Catholics, also studied at Queen's in the sixties and afterwards was a lecturer there. But in my day Catholics were thin on the ground and it seemed a pretty alien place in other ways too. Many of the academics were English, often Oxbridge, and there was a large contingent of students who were ex-service men, much older, maturer and wealthier than me.

The University is located in the most agreeable part of Belfast, near the Botanic Gardens and the Ulster Museum, an area where the wealthy people live, where religious affiliation is not a matter of concern and where harmony has reigned during the darkest times.

The main building is a formidable tudor-style structure with a tall entrance tower. I found it a little intimidating when I went to enrol. Inside along the cloisters around the quadrangle there was a crowd of young men and women hurrying about and all looking very sure of themselves. Eventually I found the right office, where I filled in a form and I was then told to wait outside a room with a number of others. We were called in one at a time and I was the last to be called. Inside were two men in academic gowns. They spent a long time going over my qualifications and at one stage I thought I was going to be turned down. But in the end they decided I could be accepted.

I was enrolled for a general arts degree which involved the study of a number of subjects over three years, a reasonable enough if not a thrilling prospect. But in the first year the subjects I was allocated were history, Latin and, incredibly, mathematics. I do not think that mathematics is an arts subject and I cannot understand why someone who did so badly in mathematics at school should have been expected to study it at university. But it was made clear that it was either that or nothing. I don't suppose the university operates such a course today but maybe someone with access to the records could provide me with an explanation for that strange decision.

Had I been older or wiser I would have withdrawn at that point before I had handed over the fee, but somehow the prospect of returning home never struck me as feasible. Maybe I even believed that I could cope with the mathematics.

Much of what happened during that year I seem to have erased from my memory. I know I did my best during the first term, attending all the lectures and doing all the assignments – even those in mathematics, though it made no sense to me. My greatest handicap was lack of money. The five shillings my mother allowed me was just enough to cover my small basic needs. I could not afford to buy text books and had to make do with those in the university library.

It was difficult to work in my lodgings. As the days shortened it became very cold in my bedroom so I would sit before the fire in the kitchen with my landlady and her father. To be fair to them they kept very quiet if I was writing. There was a front sitting-room and I don't think it ever occurred to my landlady that I might want to study there. But she was quite a kindly person and would sometimes take me with her to the cinema, especially if it was a scary film. While my studies in the kitchen were not exactly rewarding I achieved my first publishing success from there. I submitted a short essay on the Northern Irish situation for a competition in a Dublin newspaper and won a prize of a guinea. I also wrote a short story which I sent to a little weekly magazine. It was returned with a nice letter of rejection. Even that pleased me.

Despite a shortage of funds I put some effort into having a social life during that first term. At rag week I volunteered to be a collector and raised a respectable sum for charity, and I went to see the university rugby team play at Ravenhill, even though I didn't understand the game – and still don't. But in the main I gravitated towards Catholic activities which were free and with which I felt comfortable. At the weekends there was always some event at Aquinas Hall, a residence hall for Catholic women: recitals, plays, lectures, dances even whist drives. I always went to these.

I also joined the Legion of Mary, an organisation founded in Dublin in 1921, with the aim of converting the world to Catholicism. It is still, as far as I know, active and, with an aim like that, would have some way to go. One of its most spectacular actions in the early days was closing down a famous red light district in Dublin. I think they would have their work cut out in today's Dublin. Nothing like that occurred during my time in the organisation. To be honest, I just went along for the company and the chance of a good argument during the debates. My memory of the others is that they were kind, lively and surprisingly liberal-minded people.

To a generation of students whose social activities would encompass consuming large quantities of alcohol and bedding fellow students, my extra-mural life must seem pathetic, possibly bizarre. I would not quarrel with that assessment too much.

When I went home at Christmas I still retained some optimism about my studies and I said nothing to my parents that could make them doubt that they had done the right thing. But after I returned to Belfast my circumstances began to deteriorate. I had a long illness which I could never quite shake off. I had assumed it was flu but I now know it was something more sinister. And I was coming to realise that my studies were going nowhere. I gave up attending the mathematics lectures and when I felt like it would skip the others as well. I was now leading a Dostoyevskian existence: a poor student with no close friends, neglecting his studies, often spending the day just wandering around Belfast. It would have been nice to have met an equally poor young woman who would have understood my predicament and helped me to find redemption. But Belfast was not St. Petersburg.

One Sunday in the Spring my father came down to attend a Gaelic football match. He called at the house and had dinner with us. Afterwards he asked me tentatively if I would like to accompany him to the match. I think he sensed that I might have some reservations. But I thought I ought to go with him. He looked so vulnerable in his worn suit and crumpled hat. His shoes were always well polished. As we walked to the ground he asked me how I was getting on. I told him I was getting on all right but I would dearly have loved to have told him the truth about my situation. Yet I could not bring myself to do so. It would have upset him and he would not have known how to respond. We had never really been out on our own together since the time we worked on the allotment. We did not say much else. Once or twice he pointed out a house or a shop and told me who lived there in a shy way as if he felt I might not be much interested. He came alive during the match and would grin at me whenever our team got a point. At half time we went to the back of the stand and had a pee together. He lit a cigarette and as he was putting the packet away he hesitated and asked me if I would like one. I would smoke occasionally but could not bring myself to take one from him. I cannot honestly remember whether our team won or lost. After we got back to the house and had a cup of tea I said I would walk with him to the bus station. I think we said even less this time. My life might have been different if we could have communicated better.

As the year wore on I gradually came to the conclusion that it would be a waste of time and money for me to continue at University. Leaving aside mathematics I was also doing poorly in Latin and History. I believed I would fail in the end of the year examinations but, even if I had scraped through, I did not want to carry on for a further two years.

At registration I was vaguely aware that I had been allocated a personal tutor. I had never met him, but towards the end of the final term he sent me a message asking me to call and see him.

He was a very pleasant urbane man, English of course. He invited me to sit down in an armchair. He may even have offered me a sherry. He asked me how my studies were going.

When I said not very well he did not seem overly concerned. Then he made an extremely fatuous suggestion. He said: "You should go away for a short break before the exams". I thanked him for the suggestion. Outside his office I must have laughed, or grimaced at any rate. I have often thought about that piece of advice and wondered if he had in mind a Chekhovian world in which, during that short break, I would stroll along the promenade of some smart seaside resort and perhaps even meet that charming woman and her little dog.

At the end of the year I sat the examinations, even the one in mathematics. Soon after I came home I told my parents I did not want to go back. Strangely enough they did not seem too bothered. Maybe they sensed that I was not happy there or it may have been hard sending that pound every week. I never found out the results of my examination but I did get a card from the university stating that I would be expected to do better during my second year; so they did not reject me.

I had made up my mind what I would do. I had been told or had read that in England it was possible for someone with my qualifications to find a job as a teacher in a small private school. Jean was now married to Kevin, a young man from Enniskillen, and they and their little daughter, Angela, were living in Farnborough, Hampshire. I knew that they would put me up until I found something. Of course my mother was not happy when I told her of my plan but I was adamant that that I would go to England. Rita was coming for a holiday in late summer and I would go back with her.

During those months at home I developed a very annoying pain between my shoulder blades. I asked a chemist I knew if he could suggest a reason for it but he thought there was nothing to worry about. After a while it went away.

But one very pleasant event took place during this time. I received a letter from one of the Legion of Mary girls – a kind, ebullient person whose company always raised my spirits — inviting me to a picnic with the group. She wrote: "You do not need to bring anything except your sweet self". I could not refuse. We met at the station in Belfast, took the train to Strangford and then the ferry to Portaferry. Some of the group had brought food and lemonade. It was a beautiful sunny day and everyone was in such good spirits. I can still remember the happiness I felt. The others all came from well-off families and would continue at University and no doubt then enjoy comfortable middle-class lives. But that did not bother me as I had my own dream. I did not tell them that I would not see them again.

Rita came home and the days passed quickly. My mother gave me some money to buy a new jacket and a pair of trousers. I had my photograph taken for the travel identity card which was then required. I still have it and I look pretty gaunt. The day before we left I packed my few belongings in an old suitcase. My mother would now give me a sad look whenever she saw me.

Before we left I went round to the neighbours to say goodbye. My father came home to see us off. I kissed my mother and I could feel the tears on her cheek. We stopped at the corner of our street and waved. As the bus went past I could see her standing at the door . It was a scene that would be repeated many times in future years.

FOUR

The first few months in England were probably the most critical in my life. At times I wonder if those strange events were just figments of my imagination or perhaps one of those bizarre dreams to which I am now prone.

It began well enough. Farnborough may not be the most memorable of English towns but at the time I found it very congenial. I liked the streets of redbrick houses with flower gardens in front, the parks with trees and wooden benches, the modest orderly shops and the general atmosphere of tranquillity. The inhabitants were not over friendly by the standards I was used to, but they were polite and helpful and kept any religious prejudices they might have well concealed.

I was full of hope when I came to Farnborough. I was warmly welcomed by Jean and Kevin, who were kindhearted, easygoing, and encouraging and I quickly felt at ease with them and my little niece, Angela. It seemed possible that I could have a reasonable future.

As soon as I had settled in I wrote to the education agencies for lists of jobs. I also kept an eye on advertisements in the Catholic papers, *The Universe* and *The Catholic Herald*. There seemed to be a great many jobs for which I would be eminently suitable. I wonder why I never sat down and seriously considered what it would be like to work in one of those little private schools. Could I really have coped with all the petty snobbery of everyone: teachers, parents, pupils? And did I never think of something as basic as games? I must surely have known that they would have played cricket and rugby, the rules of which were a mystery to me and which I would be expected to coach. Probably my head was still stuffed with the verse of Sir Henry Newbolt and the glory of perishing at dawn in the hills of Afghanistan while remembering home and school in England. Sir Henry Newbolt has a lot to answer for.

All I got from my applications were rejections. Except once. I was asked to an interview at a small Catholic preparatory school somewhere in the Home Counties. It took me ages to get to the place, travelling across country by train and then a long walk from the station. I remember sitting down to tea with the family: the headmaster, his wife, and teenage son and daughter. It was very civilised. I could see that they belonged to a different world from mine, one that was confident, good mannered, that knew the proper way to eat. I wondered afterwards what they thought of me, that kindly man and his wife and those polite children. What did they make of my strange accent and unacceptable clothes? I am sure they would have said only nice things about me. I did not get the job.

I began to despair. I had no money and depended on the unremitting kindness of Jean and Kevin. It never seemed to have occurred to me to look for any other work than teaching. But jobs were scarce then. There were no supermarkets where I might have found casual work. And then I was also ill – in fact very ill – for a lot of the time. I sometimes forget about that when remembering my behaviour at the time. I would have frequent pains in my head and chest. I always felt very tired and there would be bouts of fever that lasted for several days. When I went to a doctor during one of those bouts I would invariably be prescribed codeine.

There was one other option with which I began to toy. At grammar school we would have regular visits from members of religious orders attempting to attract new recruits. They were very persuasive. They told us of the hazards of missionary life, the struggles against nature and the opposition of unbelieving natives, but also the rewards of building new hospitals and schools in the wilderness, of leading poor and unfortunate people from the darkness of paganism into the light of truth. It was inspiring stuff. I don't recall anyone taking up the invitation but I think it was an idea that we all kept at the back of our minds. In my mind it was moving towards the front.

At that time Catholicism in England was in a buoyant mood. The second spring that Cardinal Newman had prophesied seemed to be at hand. Converts were coming into the church by the cartload. Every year the Catholic papers would publish statistics showing the startling increase in the number of Catholics. There was a strong belief that if things went on as they were going England would again become a Catholic country.

I liked the Catholic church in England. It was more progressive and liberal and intellectual than the church in Ireland. In the world of literature Catholics like Greene and Waugh were hailed as the outstanding novelists of the day. There were lesser people too: Bruce Marshall, Compton

Mackenzie, A.J. Cronin. We seemed to have cornered the market. We had great theologians too: men like Monsignor Ronald Knox and Father Martin Darcy S.J. could more than hold their own against the best the secular world could throw at them. I had a very high opinion of these two priests. Knox translated the Bible and would frequently lecture on the radio and I would listen with bated breath, never quite comprehending what he was saying. Darcy wrote brilliant works of theology; his portrait had been painted by Augustus John and he had been photographed by Yousef Karsh.

Perhaps because of these matters, perhaps because I was desperate to find work, and perhaps also because I was weakened by illness, I asked myself if I might not find a home in the Church. I had seen advertisements placed by religious orders crying out for new recruits. I wanted something that would be exciting and worthwhile. There were religious orders dedicated to answering the spiritual and medical needs of poor people in pagan lands and I thought that one of those might suit me.

Farnborough had a boarding school for boys conducted by the Salesian Order, who were also responsible for the parish church we attended. The parish priest was an elderly, kindly man and I decided to go and ask his advice. I did not tell Jean and Kevin of my intentions. They probably would have thought that I had become a bit unstable. So one evening I went down and knocked on the door of the presbytery which was opened by a young man whom I would later get to know well. He was one of those rootless people who attached themselves to religious institutions where they do odd jobs for a pittance. I asked if I might see the parish priest and I was ushered into the parlour, one of those bleak rooms with a couple of reproductions of Italian religious paintings. The parish priest came in, shook hands with me and asked what he could do to help. He had a benign smile and a soft voice.

Of course I cannot now remember what I said but no doubt it was some waffle about me thinking I had a vocation to the priesthood. It is perfectly possible that at the time I did genuinely believe I had a vocation. I might point out that nowadays the church likes to say, in a spirit of humility, that all work is a vocation, even that of a humble housewife and mother. The religious life is only one among many vocations. Well, actually, I don't think they really quite believe that. But certainly in the 1950s they did not believe it. A call to the religious life was a very special call. It came direct from God. You would know when you had it. You might fight it but it wouldn't go away.

The parish priest listened to my faltering attempt at explaining my situation, and then he said something that I didn't quite expect. "Why don't you come in here for a while and see how you like us?" It was put in such a way that it was very hard to say no. I mean, what could I lose? It was progress. I had found a place where I was wanted. "You'll be under no obligation. I'll have a word with Rector" the priest said. So I came back the following day and met the Rector. He was a different kettle of fish. He was smooth, urbane, exuding authority, but at the same time had a kindly manner. What you would expect the Pope to be like. Before I knew it, it was all arranged: I would go in on Sunday evening.

I don't remember what Jean and Kevin said. They were probably dumbfounded. At some stage I must have written to my parents. I am not sure they would have been all that happy about it. My mother was probably perceptive enough to know that I could never make a priest.

Did I experience trepidation on my way down to the college that Sunday evening with my little suitcase? I think so. But then I thought I am going to join a company of priests. These men are close to God. They are good and loving. I will experience goodness and love. Why, I may even have been looking forward to it.

Supper had finished when I arrived. The priests were walking around the grounds in groups. The Rector had his own little group of close associates, including an elderly priest who was the bursar. They welcomed me graciously and I was introduced to other priests, all of whom seemed pleasant enough men. The Rector then called over a young man whom he introduced as Brother Michael. I cannot remember the actual name, but Michael will do. He was asked to show me my accommodation. Before we set off the Rector handed me an envelope on which was written in neat handwriting "Horarium for Mr. Whelan". I followed Brother Michael into one of the buildings and then up the stairs to a dormitory where there were about twenty beds quite close together with a locker alongside each.

Along one wall were a number of cubicles partitioned by curtains. I was shown into one of these. Inside there was a bed, a small chest of drawers and a chair. This was my accommodation. Brother Michael pointed out the toilets and showers and left me to sort myself out. I sat down on the chair and opened the envelope. It contained a folded sheet of foolscap paper again with the heading "Horarium for Mr. Whelan" and underneath the following:

6.00	Rise
6.30	Mass and sacristy
8.00	Breakfast
8.20-8.45	Serve Community at breakfast
9.30-10.00	Sacristy
10.00-12.00	Teaching or private study
12.00	Dinner
12.30	Serve Community at dinner
2.00-4.00	Teaching or private study
4.00	Tea
4.15-4.30	Serve Community at tea
5.30-7.00	Sacristy and private study
7.00	Supper
7.30	Serve Community at supper
8.30	Night prayers and sacristy
9.30	Retire

I believe that I got from this the impression that I was not there just to have a look around the place. Of course I did not expect them to take me in and feed me for nothing. I was prepared to do some work - sweep the leaves, help with the washing up or sort out the books in the library. This was giving me a different message. I wasn't just a casual guest. This was the real thing. I was in the machinery. Once again it seemed that I had got myself into a situation that had not turned out as I expected. On the other hand having just arrived and been welcomed with some genuine – if discreet – warmth, it would have been difficult to just get up and go.

Had I been serious about joining a religious order I don't think I would have chosen the Salesians. They did not have the glamour that still clings to some of the older religious orders. Unlike the Jesuits they never had among their ranks men like Mateo Ricci or Gerald Manley Hopkins. And certainly no-one like the Dominicans' Thomas Acquinas or Torquemada. They were founded in the nineteenth century by St.John Bosco for the training of youth. It was not quite what I had in mind.

In the college at that time there were about a dozen priests and three brothers. Apart from two priests who did parish work, the others taught in the school. On the whole– with one or two exceptions – they were good and kindly men. But they lead restricted lives, hedged in by petty restrictions. At meals the rector would sometimes reprimand them over eating habits. When they went out they were given a small allowance to cover fares and a modest meal. But their lives were not uncomfortable. They all had pleasant rooms – not monkish cells. The food was excellent, cooked by nuns, many of them Italian, who lived in a convent in the college grounds. At the main meals there were always jugs of beer on the table and on feast days wine was served.

The nuns were a self-effacing group. There were about eight of them all packed into a small house. I don't know what amenities they had but they could not have been lavish. Unlike the priests they did not go out and I would sometimes do shopping for them. When I passed them in the grounds they would give me a modest smile: they would never of course stop for a chat. You were not admitted into the convent. There was a rotating drum outside in which you left messages and other items for the nuns. One of the things you left was laundry. They must have been very holy people, otherwise I cannot imagine how they could have coped with washing the dirty clothes of a dozen or so men who, in those days, might not have been overly fussy about hygiene. Recently when I was in Farnborough I had a walk through the college grounds and there were no signs of the convent. It is not hard to see why.

In addition to the priests there were three brothers, two of them young men preparing for the priesthood. Brother Michael lived on the same floor as me and had similar accommodation. He was a breezy man who was given to bursts of Gilbert and Sullivan and seemed to be enthusiastic about his future. I did not particularly like him. He once thought it hilariously funny because I referred to a prie-dieu as a kneeler. For a time he went around telling other people about it and laughing his head off. The other young brother was a gentle person of whom I have good memories. There was also an elderly brother who was retired. I also liked him but he was treated with suspicion by some of the priests as he was a confidant of the Rector's and was believed to tell tales.

I found it hard to get up at six in the morning. I washed quickly and hurried down to the sacristy. It was important to get the sacristy opened early as a very old priest would always celebrate mass at 6.30. He never appeared at any other time. I would stay in the rectory until eight, serving mass for most of that time. Each of the priests would celebrate mass every morning.

In the refectory I sat with the three brothers at a small table apart from the priests. Once I had finished and cleared the table away, I looked after the priests who sat at a long table. I was helped by a young layman, another one of those people who attach themselves to religious institutions. The main meals were all formal, three course affairs. During luncheon and dinner one of the young brothers would stand at a lectern and read from a pious book. I suppose you might feel less guilty at enjoying such excellent food by listening to some dreary text being read.

During my time there the reading was from the life of Bishop Challoner, an eighteenth century Catholic prelate. Once, when I was clearing up after lunch, I accidentally knocked the book off the lectern and then put it back open at the wrong place – again by accident. At dinner the reader was Brother Michael and he got into a great fluster as he tried to find the right place, causing his audience some amusement. Afterwards he accused me of being responsible and I vigorously denied the charge. It took him a while to get over it and he would bring the matter up from time to time. Well, brother, if you're still around and might chance to read this, I would like to come clean. It was my fault and I am sorry. But I don't feel it was one of the sins crying out to heaven for vengeance. Probably no worse than singing Gilbert and Sullivan.

The Rector wanted me to improve my Latin. Although it was one of my best subjects he got it into his head that it was my weakest. I was given a Latin class to teach and at the same time was told to study the subject privately. I quite enjoyed teaching Latin, using the ever faithful *Longman's Latin Grammar*. I would always study the lesson a day in advance. Whether these middle-class English boys understood my accent I could never be sure. In the evenings I would supervise their private study. It was the best part of my time in the College. I was less keen on serving in the refectory.

Gradually my illness began to get worse. I would get high

temperatures and frequent headaches. I always felt cold. So cold that I could only give myself a cursory wash in the mornings. It was an effort to shave. I don't think I could have smelled great. Sometimes after lunch I would go up to the dormitory to rest for a few minutes and would fall asleep. When I awoke my class would be almost over and I would have to make profuse apologies to the priest who had filled in for me. Of course, when I felt very ill I was sent off to the doctor who would invariably diagnose flu. Then for a time I would have a respite.

One Saturday I was sent out on an errand, and as I was going along the road, I saw, coming towards me in the distance, one of the boys I taught, accompanied by his parents. I could see that he had spotted me and was telling his parents. I was dirty, unshaven and dishevelled. Maybe they would have excused me as an eccentric. But I could not face them. I just turned and crossed the road and did not look back. I don't know what my poor little pupil must have thought of me but he looked at me strangely when we met in class.

The school term came to an end and I said goodbye to my Latin class. Something very touching happened. As I was walking away from the classroom, one of the boys came running after me calling "Sir, Sir". He was the boy who had given me the most trouble in the class. Not disruptive trouble, he just seemed unable to grasp what I was trying to put over. He was panting from running. He handed me an envelope and ran off again. Inside was a Christmas card which he had drawn for me and on which he had written: "Sorry for all the trouble I gave". I wanted to cry. Perhaps I did.

Shortly before Christmas the Rector summoned me to his

room. He had quite a modest room, part of which was used as an office. There was a screen in front of his bed. He told me he had various reports about me, some of them good, some bad. I think by now we both knew that the priestly life was not for me. But he was a kindly man and he said I could stay on at the college until I could find a job. I could continue working in the sacristy and serving mass and possibly help in the bursar's office. If I wanted to lodge in the college he could give me a small weekly allowance but, if I wanted to stay with my sister, he would give me a little more. I would no longer have to teach or serve in the refectory but could still have my meals along with the other lay people. I thanked him for the offer and accepted it gladly. When I told Jean and Kevin they too were pleased.

After I moved back to their house, one of my first acts was to get into the bath where I soaked for a long time. I had Christmas dinner at the college, with the same excellent food served to the priests but in a more modest setting, and in the jollier company of the motley group of hangers-on. We played music and danced and I felt happier than I had for what seemed a very long time.

Of course my troubles were not over. I still had to get up at six in the morning to open the sacristy for the aged priest. But this time instead of walking a few yards across the quadrangle I now had to walk half a mile on dark winter mornings, sometimes through rain and snow. Once only, I think, did I sleep in and leave the aged priest in a distressed state.

Although my illness was getting worse and I was now coughing up blood, I was still determined to find a job as a teacher. What was more I could now claim that I had taught in a prestigious school. Once again I wrote off to the agencies for lists of jobs and sent off applications. Sometime in February, what I thought was a breakthrough took place. I had a letter from a school in Surbiton asking me to come for an interview. I remember the day I went quite well. I felt very ill, probably had a high temperature, and yet I was so enthusiastic about the possibility of a job. The headmaster, a youngish man, welcomed me. He was pleased that I had been educated by the Christian Brothers as he had employed former brothers as teachers and thought they were good. He showed me around the school and explained my duties. In addition to teaching, I would take the boys for games. So keen was I to get a job that I told him this would not present a problem.

Afterwards we went into his sitting room for tea and a young woman joined us, sitting down on the sofa beside me. She was an extremely good-looking woman. Unusually for the period she had bare legs and this seemed to me to be very sexually attractive. I can still recall her white smooth knees and the very faint down on her legs, and her subtle perfume. She was extremely friendly and yet I am sure I must have been a sorry sight. She told me casually and not in a superior way that she had been to finishing school in Switzerland. I suppose I was a bit bedazzled by her. I went back with the headmaster to his office and he told me he was offering me the job. He would like me to come on Sunday so that I could start work on Monday. I think now he must have been very desperate to find a teacher, though at the time I probably believed he had been impressed by me. Anyway, I accepted his offer without hesitation. I have no recollection of the pay or even my accommodation but these matters would not have bothered me too much. I was just thrilled to be offered a job.

As the headmaster walked with me down the drive we met a middle-aged, rather severe-looking woman whom he introduced to me as the school matron. When he told her that I was joining the staff, I noticed that she raised her eyebrows a little but thought nothing of it then.

On the train back to Farnborough I suppose I indulged in some ridiculous dreams, perhaps of a love affair with the beautiful woman with the bare legs. How foolish I must have been to have accepted the job. I must surely have known that I would ultimately have hated living in that little school and have been totally unable to cope with coaching cricket and rugby; even surely aware that the young woman, however well-mannered, would probably have despised me.

When I got back and told Jean and Kevin they expressed concern about my health and wondered if I was wise to start working until I felt better. But I was determined that I would go. I need not have worried. The following morning I received a telegram from the headmaster which said simply: "Do not come. Writing". It was a blow. In a way it did not matter too much as I felt so ill that day that I had to go to bed, and I was to stay there for a long time.

The headmaster never did write. He probably could not think of a satisfactory excuse for his behaviour. I expect the matron, after taking one look at me, had realised that I was not too long for this world and had passed on the message. I can understand why the headmaster changed his mind but I still think that it was cowardly of him not to write.

The following week I stayed in bed and Jean got a doctor to come and examine me. He was the first doctor who had an inkling of what was the matter with me. He promised to come back and do further tests. But at the weekend Rita came down from London and she too was very worried by my condition. She told the nuns in the private hospital where she worked about me and they agreed that I should come up to the hospital so that one of the doctors could examine me.

At the hospital I was put in a small ward with a number of men, all of whom had problems requiring surgery. I think they looked at me with suspicion. They were paying a lot of money and they must have noticed from my faded old pyjamas that I was not too prosperous. But once I was in the bed I felt fine. I know now that Rita was very worried about me and I expect it irritated her that I was so cheerful.

I was weighed and found to be only seven stone, about four stone less that I should have been. When the doctor examined me he recommended that I should go to the local clinic for an X-ray. Rita came along with me. The results of the X-ray were not good but then not altogether unexpected. We spoke to the doctor in the clinic who told me I had tuberculosis in both lungs. To be honest I was not greatly worried, probably just relieved that at last they had discovered the cause of my illness. The doctor explained, as Rita probably knew, that there was nothing he could do for me. Today, of course, I could have immediately gone into hospital and received treatment. But in Britain in the 1940s tuberculosis was very prevalent. Thousands of people were dying from it every year. Hospitals and sanatoria specialising in tuberculosis were bursting at the seams. Many of the patients were ex-service men who had contracted the disease from the harsh conditions during their war service. There was no possibility of my getting a bed in a hospital in Britain. My only option was to return home where I would not survive for very long. It seems overly dramatic to say this now, but it was true.

When I went back to the hospital I was put in a private room to avoid contact with the other patients. It was a wonderful room and the food was delicious. I don't think I ever thanked the nuns properly for their kindness. An elderly nun was in charge of newspaper distribution and she felt that The *Daily Mirror* was the most appropriate paper for me. I had no objections to that. However when the chaplain, a pompous young man, came to see me he told me, that in his opinion, the *Daily Mirror* was not suitable reading for a good Catholic. I kept reading it, anyway.

Now I had to write to my mother and inform that I had tuberculosis and would be coming home. This was an easier task for me than for Rita as I was feeling fine. In fact I did not realise for a long time afterwards just how seriously ill I was. The doctor had told Rita but she did not pass it on to me. I am grateful to her for that as it was a heavy burden for her to bear. I do not remember what I wrote to my mother or what she said in reply. I probably did not even realise what a massive shock for my parents it would have been.

Rita had planned to travel home with me and had booked berths on the ferry and seats on the train to Heysham. We would get a taxi to Euston Station. Then on the morning of our departure, as we were preparing to leave, a strange thing happened. Were I a more devout Catholic I would have called it a miracle.

This was the set up. The taxi had arrived outside the hospital and we said goodbye to the kind nuns. Just as we were going through the door the telephone in the office rang.

The call was for Rita. It was from the doctor at the clinic. He had managed to find me a bed in Colindale Hospital in North London, a hospital that was pioneering new treatments for tuberculosis. Was I willing to go there? It was not a difficult question to answer. I owe so much to this Englishman, whose name I do not even remember, who did not know me, but who had been moved by my plight and had gone to a great deal of trouble to find me a place in hospital. And he was someone else I never properly thanked. I have asked myself many times if there could have been a reason for this last minute reprieve. I can think of nothing in my subsequent life that would appear to justify it. Why was George Orwell, who was then at the height of his creative powers and who would die from tuberculosis the following year, not saved?

I went back to my room to await the transfer to Colindale Hospital and wrote home again to give my parents the good news. My mother may not have been all that pleased. She probably had not realised how seriously ill I was and would, no doubt, have been happy to look after me herself.

A week later I was taken by ambulance to Colindale Hospital. The hospital is an uncompromising Victorian building that on the outside gives no indication of the human drama being played out within. I would spend a year there, one of the happiest periods of my life.

I was put in Ward 2, which had about twenty beds, all of them occupied. A sanatorium is different from other hospitals, or was in those days. Most of the patients will have been there a long time and a camaraderie will have been built up over the weeks and months. The arrival of a new patients arouses some interest. There is a little concern about whether he will fit in smoothly or whether he will be a pain. I don't think I gave any cause for concern.

After I had been X-rayed and examined I was given the treatment used in severe cases. This meant being confined to bed and to lying flat on my back for a couple of weeks. I did not like the experience much as it involved the use of a bedpan, an experience that was not made more pleasant as the orderly, a tall, witty Lithuanian, would look over the screen to check on my performance. It was also decided that I should be given a course of streptomycin, a new drug that had recently come in from the United States and was being used on a trial basis in a couple of hospitals in Britain. I was one of the first people to be treated with it.

Streptomycin saved my life and I owe a debt of gratitude to those who discovered it. Its discovery is generally attributed to Selman Abraham Waksman, who was born in July 1888 to Jewish parents in a peasant village near Kiev in the Ukraine – I think of him being knouted by a passing Cossack - and who emigrated to the United States in 1910, where he had a distinguished academic career, leading to the award of the Nobel Prize. His research was responsible for the discovery of several antibiotics – a term he himself coined – among them Streptomycin in 1944. One of Waksman's research students, Albert Schalz, later claimed that it was he who made the discovery, but he had been working in Waksman's laboratory, using Waksman's techniques and under Waksman's direction. Whatever the truth of the matter, I offer the spirits of them both my humble thanks.

The treatment lasted for six months and involved intramuscular injections in my thighs or buttocks every six hours. I finished up with a lot of bruises but that was a small matter to complain about. Every morning the doctor came round and looked at each patient's chart. He was a rather surly man, not given much to chat, but he did exude confidence which was what mattered. One day after I had been lying flat for a fortnight he looked at my chart as usual then handed it back to the sister and was passing on when he hesitated, came back, gave the tiniest of smiles and said "I think you can sit up now". I knew then that the Streptomycin was working and that I was recovering.

A nurse or an orderly would now push me in a wheelchair to the toilet and it was very pleasant to be able to get out and sit down there on my own. In hospital such little things like that become so important.

Now that I could sit up in bed I had more contact with my fellow patients. On the whole they were such good people. Even when they knew they would never recover they did not complain. They would still joke, help each other with a crossword, flirt with the nurses. I have such fond memories of them and of their goodness.

There was such a contrast between the atmosphere in the hospital and that in the college. Why did there seem to be so much more genuine love and concern for one's fellow human beings here where very few would have any strong religious belief? When I went to the college I think I naively expected to feel that same warmth that I was now experiencing in the hospital. It has always seemed to me strange that religious establishments can be so cold and sterile and harsh while they preach the importance of loving one another. I am sure that the theologians will have an answer.

Not long after I went into hospital my mother came over to England. She went to Farnborough to stay with Jean and

Kevin and on the Sunday after her arrival she came to see me. I can remember well her walking down the ward, a sombre look on her face. I think she expected me to look as if the Angel of Death had passed over me. It took a few more weekend visits before she was sure that I might recover. Jean and Rita had come with her on that first visit but after that she was able to make the journey on her own, negotiating the underground without difficulty.

She stayed for a few months until I was able to walk around and meet her in the day room. My father meanwhile was getting a bit restless at home with no one to cook for him or wash his clothes. For the only time in his life he wrote me a letter naturally expressing concern about my health but also explaining how much he missed my mother. It was clearly the action of a desperate man. Eventually Rita went home for a time to look after his needs.

Life was never dull in the hospital. There was always lively conversation with those around us. We had newspapers; I had now graduated to the *News Chronicle*. One of the patients did *The Times* crossword and we would do our best to help out. We listened to the radio on headphones. I don't know what stations existed in 1948 but we always listened to the Home Service. In the mornings most of us would listen to Housewives Choice. In the evenings the great attraction was the dramatised serial. The one that grabbed us particularly was *King Solomon's Mines*. There would be silence throughout the ward when that was on. The Red Cross brought round a trolley of books every week but I never found it easy to read a book in hospital. Occasionally there would a film show, nothing too demanding, often a Laurel and Hardy film. A television set was brought in once so that we could see a boxing match.

But somehow the simple routines of hospital seemed to take up the day. We were woken at six o'clock when the night staff would bring a cup of tea and get you washed before they went off duty. Then there was breakfast. After breakfast we could smoke for half an hour. If you were caught smoking after that you were severely reprimanded. It seems strange now that smoking was then allowed in a sanatorium. Then there was the ward round which lasted a long time. You were always wondering what the doctor was going to tell you. It was a bit like having your homework marked at school. Like school not everyone got a good mark. Someone who was thought to be doing well might be told to have complete rest again. We always felt sorry when that happened, and at the same time, glad that it had not happened to us.

After lunch there was occupational therapy. The occupational therapist was an extremely charming and attractive young woman. Had I been in good health, older, wealthier and bolder I might have tried my luck with her. She seemed to think I was a person with some culture as she would converse with me about books and films. Once she confessed to me in a very confidential manner that she had been greatly shocked by the immoral behaviour in a foreign film she had just seen and I found that very touching. At first she had me making little stuffed rabbits which I gave to Jean and Kevin for Angela but when I became mobile she arranged for me to work in what was termed the printing department. This was located in a little shed and comprised one small pedal-operated printing press. However, there was a genuine printer who instructed me in setting type by hand and operating the machine. This experience would stand me in good stead in my subsequent careers.

The Borough of Lambeth, where Rita's hospital was located, took an interest in my welfare and I had a visit from a member of staff who suggested I might like to take up a correspondence course during the remainder of my time in hospital. This would be funded by the Borough. By this time I had abandoned any thoughts of becoming a teacher or a priest but I had now begun to cherish hopes that I might be a writer. So I chose a course in short story writing, but after a couple of lessons I decided I did not want to continue. I found the idea of being taught how to write embarrassing. Great writers, I realised, did not take correspondence courses. I transferred to a course for the London University matriculation examination which I enjoyed. The mathematics which I had found so difficult at school now seemed surprisingly easy. When eventually I sat the examination I got excellent results.

Most of the men in the ward had been in the forces during the war and I liked to hear them talk of their experiences. Two who were in beds near me had been prisoners of war, one in Germany, the other in Japan. The former had escaped, made it to Poland where he had an affair with a Polish woman, but had then been recaptured. They were both very ill and I am sure would not have survived for long.

Next to me was another ex-soldier, a Catholic of Irish origin. We became very friendly. I remember we both listened on the radio to an account of the celebrations in Dublin when the Irish Free State was declared a republic. At the end of the broadcast he gave me a thumbs up salute. He made a great mistake in becoming infatuated with a very young nurse who for a time responded to his advances. But when she left the ward she broke off all contact with him. It hit him very hard and when months later I was discharged, he was still very bitter about it. He, too, was very ill.

Most of the wards had balconies open to the elements where patients who were fit enough could volunteer to move. There was space for only two beds on a balcony so it was important to have an agreeable companion. One of those who moved out was an evangelical Christian called Denis who had been getting into a little trouble with his companion in the ward, a belligerent non-believer. Denis could not help bearing witness to his strong beliefs and that would involve contradicting any unorthodox opinions when they were expressed. No one wanted to share the balcony with Denis so I volunteered to do so. He was a kind but very difficult man who probably thought that, despite my strongly held Christian views, I was nevertheless on the way to hell. So I had to pick my words carefully when I spoke to him. Theological debate was quite out of the question. Although at the time I had a strong faith I was open to the occasional moment of doubt, but Denis was forever the single-minded pilgrim heading straight for glory. His wife came to see him every Sunday, an equally kind and unswerving believer. Once, probably to assure him that RCs did read the Bible, I showed him the Douay New Testament that I had been given in the college. But he made no comment, doubtless considering that translation to be the work of Beelzebub. When I left he gave me a copy of the King James Bible, on the flyleaf of which he had written: "To Tony, with Christian remembrances from Denis" together with quotations from John and Timothy. He was a good man.

My health continued to improve dramatically and I put on several stone in weight. When my mother felt assured that I would recover she returned home. After six months I was allowed out to walk around the grounds of the hospital and later on at the weekends I could go into London. On these occasions I was usually accompanied by George, another patient well on the road to recovery. George was a Londoner, a little older than me. He too had been a soldier but enlisted too late to be involved in any action. I suppose that culturally we had not too much in common but he was good-natured and easy-going and accepted that we were different. He did not mind if I went into bookshops or galleries. Before he became ill he had worked as a steward at the Royal Naval College in Greenwich. We went there one afternoon and had the pleasant experience of having tea with a couple of Wrens in the kitchen at the back of the Painted Hall. He was another good man. We corresponded for a while after we left. I should have kept up our friendship but I was a thoughtless person then.

One weekend I went down to Farnborough and stayed with Jean and Kevin. While I was there I called at the college. There was a new rector but most of the other priests were still there and I was warmly welcomed and invited to lunch. This time I sat at the main table with the priests and had my food served. There was one change to the arrangements in the refectory. The new rector did not approve of his flock drinking alcohol, and the beer had been replaced by fruit juice, not a universally popular arrangement. The bursar invited me over to his office and apologised for the fact that nobody in the community had noticed the condition of my health. He gave me five pounds as a late Christmas present. I was touched by that.

After a year in hospital and six months after the end of the

Streptomycin course I was told I was well enough to go home. It was impressed on me that I was by no means cured. I would need to have regular X-rays and check-ups and to take life easy for a very long time. I was also strongly advised to go to a rehabilitation centre such as Papworth in Cambridgeshire where I could start working gradually and under supervision.

Before I left the hospital I went back to see the doctor at the clinic in Lambeth. I remember telling him very airily that I could not have been too ill after all. He surprised me by saying that I had been very ill indeed. In fact, he had never expected to see me again.

On the afternoon just before I was leaving I went round the ward and said good-bye to other patients. I would miss them. They were such good people and I knew some of them would not be around much longer. I said goodbye also to the kind-hearted nurses and to the stern ward sister who gave me one of her infrequent smiles.

Rita went with me to Euston along with the Lithuanian orderly who had volunteered to carry my suitcase. I am sure Rita was pleased with the outcome. At the beginning I would have been an enormous burden to her. The Borough of Lambeth had kindly paid my fare and had booked a first class cabin for me on the ferry. The following morning as the ferry sailed up the Lagan I thought Belfast looked better than I could remember it, a sort of warm, homely place. The bus station was a long way from the docks and for the first time in my life I took a taxi.

As we got near Kilkeel I felt that little bit of trepidation I would always feel arriving home by bus. The bus stop was just by the corner where the men congregated and the arrival of a bus would be watched with interest. When they saw me getting off with my suitcase I knew they would look disinterested but there would be gossip about me afterwards.

I saw my father come over, a smile on his face. He would have taken the morning off. We did not shake hands. We never did anything like that. He asked if I was alright and I said I was. He carried my suitcase. As we turned the corner I saw my mother standing at the door. She would have seen the bus go by the end of the road. Some of the neighbours were standing at their doors as well and as I went past they said "You're welcome home, Anthony". My mother kissed me and we went inside. From the loving way she kept looking at me I could tell she was overjoyed to have me back. My father never said much at such times but I could sense that he too was happy.

FIVE

I spent a year at home before going to Papworth. I was X-rayed regularly and prescribed cod liver oil and malt, but otherwise I lived a normal and carefree life without the need to worry about finding a job. I was given sickness benefit of thirty shillings a week, a pound of which I passed on to my mother. I was perfectly happy with the remaining ten shillings.

My needs were very simple. Thinking back I am hard put to figure out what I spent the ten shillings on. I smoked only occasionally and I did not drink. In fact I was never in a public house in my home town until many years later: it was not then considered respectable to go into pubs.

I did go to the cinema quite frequently. There were now two cinemas in the town. During the time I was away the old cinema, which during the war was used for billets by the army, had been renovated. Whether by accident or design it showed some very poor films. I would have left early on a few occasions except that I knew the manager and I did not want to hurt his feelings.

My other main outlay was on reading matter. During the week I would usually make do with *The Irish Press* as my father liked it, but on Sunday I would buy *The Sunday Times* and *The Observer*, mainly for the book and film reviews. I also bought magazines like *The Listener* and *Picture Post*. The newsagent was a family friend who would allow me to skim through his other papers and magazines. He would also order books for me and I would pay off the cost in instalments. I had an eclectic taste and my purchases ranged from *The Pickwick Papers* to Dorothy Macardle's *The Irish Republic*. I never got through all of *The Irish Republic* but it was a big impressive book and allowed me to feel an affinity with the republican tradition in a respectable way.

The rest of my reading requirements were met by two small circulating libraries and by the parish library where I was welcomed back by the nuns. I did not tell them the full story of my encounter with the priesthood but let them think I had given up because of illness rather than a lack of enthusiasm.

I did not lead a sedentary life. In the summer I swam in the sea every day and in the autumn I joined the badminton club that had sessions twice a week in the parish hall. I got the hang of the game quickly enough, though I realised I would never be a great player. The others, who were mainly teachers and nurses, were good natured and friendly and never made me feel inadequate.

Although I had no immediate need to worry about work, I did from time to time think of what I might do with my life when I was fully recovered. I had ruled out the priesthood and the thought of teaching no longer appealed to me. And I did not want a mundane occupation.

I had developed a serious interest in the cinema. The Penguin edition of Roger Marvell's book *Cinema* became my bible. I still have the copy I bought then with passages underlined and notes in the margins. Most of the films Marvell singles out for praise I was never likely to see except in some specialist cinema in a major city. But I was now aware of the existence of Eisenstein, Pudovkin, Pabst, Murnau, Dreyer, Feyder, Clair, Vigo. I already had some acquaintance with Lang, Dieterle, Sturges and of course, John Ford, who for a long time was regarded by me as the greatest of them all. There were moments when I could see myself as a film director, smoking a cigar and remonstrating with some fabulously beautiful but temperamental actress. It was a nice dream to enjoy occasionally.

But, if deep down, I knew I would never make it as a film director, I had few doubts that I would succeed in the world of literature. At first I was not especially concerned about becoming a great writer. I was just happy to see my name in print. The first thing I had published was a piece of doggerel about the loss of a fishing boat. It appeared in a local paper to some acclaim. After that there was no stopping me.

Soon I was having articles published regularly in the local papers and in little magazines published by religious orders, for which I would get a guinea. It was easy work. We had an old set of encyclopaedias at home and I would go through these looking for ideas. It was not difficult to find them. If it was November I would find customs associated with the month and make up an article from that. The parish library was another great source of material. I wrote a series of potted biographies of great Irishmen all taken from their biographies. For a guinea you could not be expected to do original research. My literary work was not unnoticed in the neighbourhood. We had among us a gentleman who was known as The Poet. I would see him about the town always dressed in a long overcoat, sometimes pushing a bicycle, stern-faced, observant, a man akin in my eyes to the poet in Browning's *How it Strikes a Contemporary;*

> "He took such cognizance of men and things,
> If any beat a horse, you felt he saw;
> If any cursed a woman, he took note;
> Yet stared at nobody; - you stared at him
> And found, less to your pleasure and surprise,
> He seemed to know you and expect as much".

Despite his title I never came across any verse written by The Poet but doubtless there had been some apprentice pieces before he turned to prose. He was published extensively in local newspapers and publications such as *Ireland's Own*. Several booklets by him about local people and events were also published – indeed some are probably still in print. Although I never spoke to the man he knew about me. This is a story which my mother would tell with amusement. She went to a wake in The Poet's neck of the woods and the great man was there. He was a distant relation of hers. "I expect you know me" she said to him. "I don't", The Poet replied somewhat brusquely, "but I know your son. He's a writer". It is my lifelong regret that I have never been able to live up to his faith in me.

During this period I did meet and speak to another writer of a different calibre. One of the local Catholic teachers stopped me in the street one day to tell me that Michael McLaverty would be giving a talk to the teachers' group in one of the town's hotels. Knowing my interest in literature he thought I might like to attend. I was very excited at the prospect of meeting McLaverty, some of whose short stories I had read in a little volume called *The Game Cock and Other Stories* and they had made a considerable impression on me. McLaverty, who died in 1992 at the age of 88, was a teacher in Belfast for all his working life, during which he published several novels and collections of short stories. In Ireland he still enjoys a considerable reputation but his work is little known elsewhere. It is interesting in the light of subsequent events in my life that McLaverty was the first writer with whom the novelist John McGahern made contact. Their correspondence has recently been published.

I went to the meeting with some trepidation. Apart from my acquaintance I knew no-one in the audience, made up of teachers from Catholic and Protestant schools in the town. McLaverty, a slightly built and quietly spoken man, gave a brief survey of the state of literature in twentieth century Ireland, concentrating on the big names like Corkery, O'Faolain, O'Flaherty, O'Connor. When he had finished the chairman called for questions and I summoned up enough courage to ask McLaverty if he would like to devote all his time to writing. He was very dismissive of the idea. That would mean being a professional writer he told me a little scornfully. At the time I was disappointed with the answer and it lowered McLaverty in my estimation. I would have thought that the profession of writing was a noble one. But I can see now where he was going.

One other influential event occurred during my stay at home. I went to Dublin for the first time. Dublin had always been considered by northern Catholics to be the real capital but was viewed with some contempt by unionists. And I had seen articles in English newspapers describing the squalor and poverty. But I felt I ought to go and just hoped I would not be too disappointed. I found the address of a bed and breakfast establishment in *The Irish Press* and booked two nights there.

All of Ireland then was a pretty poor country but the South was poorer than the North. People were leaving in droves to go to England. On the way to Dublin the train stopped at Dundalk and Drogheda, two dreary and impoverished looking towns. Today they have been transformed and a new motorway from Dublin runs past them. The suburbs of Dublin seemed very squalid and the sight made my heart sink. Amiens Street station was so small compared with London stations and most of the people around looked poor and provincial. So I was not that happy as I walked down Talbot Street, a rough street then noted for its cheap and unsalubrious boarding houses.

But when I reached O'Connell Street my mood changed dramatically. Across that wide street and looking beautiful in the sunshine was the General Post Office where, on Easter Monday, 1916, Patrick Pearse had read the Proclamation of the Republic. Whatever reservations I had about that event and what came after it, when I saw the building and the green white and orange tricolour flying above it, I couldn't help feeling, well, a bit proud. I had no problem with Nelson's Pillar. It was tall and elegant and commemorated a hero, even if he wasn't ours. For a long time I stood looking up and down O'Connell Street, marvelling at how fine it seemed and thinking that I had been very wrong to worry that I might be disappointed. On the way to my boarding house I stopped at the monument to Charles Stewart Parnell, a fine piece of work, to read the inscription: "No man has the right to say to his nation thus far and no further. No man has the right to fix a *ne plus ultra* to the march of Irish nationhood and we never shall". All this made me glow with a patriotic fervour which, occasionally may do no great harm. Most of my life I have been a cynic.

I did the rounds of the galleries and museums. The Municipal Gallery, near to my boarding house, was a very nice building with some decent paintings. I think I was the only person in it and the attendants looked at me with a little suspicion as if they feared I might be some kind of crackpot. There was a similar lack of people in the National Gallery which had some good paintings, possibly some great paintings, and yet it also was practically empty. The same was also the case with the National Museum, then a dusty, provincial-seeming place, though I was impressed with the gold ornaments made by our ancestors all those centuries ago. At that time and, as I was to discover, for many years afterwards, the Irish people on the whole were not interested in art or antiquities. They did not mind preserving these institutions as symbols of respectability, nor to paying modest salaries to a few remote and dedicated people to look after them. Today the situation has changed for the better. Dublin's art galleries and museums have been regenerated and are generally well patronised.

Most of the time I just spent walking around the streets and going into shops, especially bookshops. That for me is still the best thing about visiting a city. I did not have much money but I did buy one book, *The Confessions of St. Augustine* which cost ten shillings. I made a few attempts to read it but never got very far. It looks good on the shelves.

One thing I had set my heart on was a visit to the Abbey Theatre. On my first morning I went to the box office of the little theatre in Abbey Street and bought the most expensive ticket I could afford for that evening's performance. The play was *Katie Roche* by Teresa Deevy, and I had never heard of either the play or its author. I think I would have been happier if It had been a work that I had known about by say O'Casey or Synge. Nevertheless I was very excited to be going.

I had a good seat near the front to which I was ushered by a charming young woman from whom I purchased one of those distinctive brown-covered Abbey programmes. It seemed wonderful to me that on that stage a few feet away the poet Yeats had berated the audience for their narrow-minded opposition to Synge's great play, *The Playboy of the Western World*. I thought the play was pretty good and excellently acted. I now know a bit more about the author, who died in 1963 at the age of sixty, and who wrote a number of plays for the Abbey, often about romantic young women in rural Ireland who are forced by circumstances to abandon their youthful illusions and accept the dullness of real life. Theresa Deevey's talent was kept in check by the narrow Catholic world of her day and she is now largely forgotten. But I remember that performance with gratitude.

I was sorry to leave Dublin. I envied those genial people with whom I shared the streets and shops and public buildings of the great city that I could also claim as mine. It struck me that it would be wonderful if one day I could live and work there.

The year at home had been a good one. There were many things that gave me much pleasure, particularly the start of my career as a writer and the visit to Dublin.. I got on so well with my parents who seemed now to have a very tranquil relationship. Sometimes we all went to the cinema together. I loved sitting in the cinema with them.

When I arrived there in 1950, Papworth Everard was a tiny village a few miles from Cambridge. It had one long street with a pub at either end, an ancient parish church, a Catholic chapel, two shops and several small factories. It also was the home of Papworth Village Settlement which began life in 1927 for the treatment of people suffering from tuberculosis. Just off the quiet village street and screened by trees were a couple of hospitals and various forms of accommodation for patients.

On arrival I was put in one of the hospitals for a few days to be checked out. On the second morning the matron came round with one of her minions. She looked at my chart for a while and then said: "Don't you think it's a bit strange when lots of our own boys need to get in here that we should bring someone over from Ireland". I made no comment. It occurred to me that Sir Basil Brooke would have not been pleased to know that an Ulsterman was not considered one of "our own boys". After she had gone the other men in the ward said they were sorry. The English are a very fair people.

After a few days I was moved up to the area known as South Park where I was given a wooden chalet, of which there were several rows. There were only men at South Park. Where the women went I don't remember. The chalets were the size of a modest garden shed and contained a bed, a chest of drawers, a table and, I think, a little electric fire. There were flaps at the side that would open up. I had a chalet at the very end of a row with just the countryside beyond. It was a long walk to the toilet block so at night those of us in end chalets would lift up the flap and pee over the side.

Life at South Park was good. There was a communal block with showers, a dining room, a lounge with a television set and a small library. During meals I sat at a table with five other men, three Englishmen, a Scot and a Liverpool Irishman. They were excellent company, very witty and good-natured. It was everything that one could ask for.

We did not sit around all day doing nothing. There were factories producing luggage and furnishings for cars and a printing works. I opted for the printing works: there were seldom any vacancies but my brief experience of printing in Colindale Hospital told in my favour. I don't know if the printing works still exists; even then it was finding the going hard. Its bread-and-butter work was for His Majesty's Stationary Office and then the most boring work produced by that organisation, endless reports filled with tables of statistics. Occasionally the manuscript of a novel would come in from the publishers, Ward Lock. It would be something pretty trashy but a welcome break, nonetheless. I tried hand composing at first but it was decided that proof-reading would be more suitable for me. There was one proof-reader already, a middle-aged woman, not a patient, who lived locally. She seemed very happy to have me as an assistant.

Mrs. James was a gracious cultured person with whom it was an enormous pleasure to work. She patiently taught me the rules of proof-reading and I was soon modestly adequate. We would take it in turn to read the proofs to one another. Sometimes I was aware that I had mispronounced a word but she made no comment. During tea breaks we would discuss books and films. She had a daughter in her early twenties, a stunningly beautiful young woman, who would come in from time to time and who was as charming and pleasant as her mother. I think that I had one of the best jobs in Papworth.

After a spell in the chalet I moved down to a hostel in the village where I shared a room with an agreeable countryman of mine, quietly spoken and with a dry wit. I lived a full life with many friends, men and women. In the evenings a few of us would walk to one of the pubs for a leisurely drink. There were weekly film shows, concerts, dances, lectures on music and art. Within walking distance were other little villages. I came to like the flat landscape. At weekends buses went to the neighbouring towns. From time to time Rita would come up to Cambridge and we would have a meal together and stroll happily about that beautiful city.

I suppose it would have been nice if I could have continued for ever in this serene way. But after I had been in the settlement for a little over a year I was aware that I would soon be discharged. In any case there were other things I wanted to do with my life. In particular I wished to return to Ireland. Although I still wrote stories and articles, my head was now bursting with grandiose ideas for producing great literary works and I had this simple view that if I was back among my own people I could succeed.

One day I was told that Mr. Grogan, the general manager of Papworth Industries, wanted to see me. I had never met Mr. Grogan but I had heard of his reputation. One of the women patients told me that he had been rude to her during an interview and had made her stand all the time. So I was a bit nervous when I walked to his office.

Mr. Grogan was a tall wiry man. He had a spacious, well furnished office. When I went in he was scrutinising a document which presumably contained my personal details.

After a time he looked up and said severely: "I see you are Irish, Whelan". I said I was. It was all right at the time to address people simply by their surnames. He told me to sit down. "Your medical report shows that you have completed your treatment and are eligible to be discharged". I agreed that that was probably the case. "What are your plans?". I said I wanted to go back to Ireland. He gave me a hard look. "There is nothing in Ireland for you". I said I wasn't sure about that. "What do you want to do?" I thought I might as well tell him the truth. "I want to write". He did not dismiss the idea. "You would still need to get a job". Then he called in his secretary and said he did not want to be disturbed. Mr. Grogan was anxious to talk about Irish literature. He asked me what Irish writers I had read. I mentioned Sean O'Faolain and Frank O'Connor. He dismissed both of them saying "I don't like people who crap in their own beds". I liked that remark, however unjust it might be to the two writers in question. He asked me if I knew Liam O'Flaherty. I said of course I did. "I served with O'Flaherty in the Irish Guards in the First World War". I did not doubt this. I think he was an honest man. I did not say O'Flaherty was also not above crapping in his own bed.

We talked about Ireland. He did most of the talking. Although he was a bit intimidating I could tell that I had found an ally. I did not dare ask him what his Irish connections were. He said confidentially: "We Irish should look after one another. They don't like us here". In his case I found that hard to credit. It was not so long since I had seen him escorting Countess Mountbatten when she came to open the village fete and they seemed to be hitting it off extremely well. You never can tell with people.

We spent a leisurely hour together. He told me he would like me to stay and he would get me a permanent job in Papworth – but not unfortunately in the printing works. I said I would think seriously about it.

I came away from Mr. Grogan feeling quite pleased. His offer was very tempting. I liked living in Papworth. I could settle there, marry one of those nice girls from the village, and have a secure happy life. But it wasn't really what I wanted. I would have to do some boring clerical job and would be trapped there forever.

I did not tell any of my friends the whole story of my meeting with Mr. Grogan, and certainly not the woman to whom he had been rude. I had a couple of letters from Mr. Grogan after I left Papworth. He gave me a reference, which he said he would never normally do. He also said he would still like me to come back to Papworth. When, twenty years later, I went on a sentimental visit to Papworth I was told he was still living there in retirement. It was suggested that I should visit him. But I declined.

I went home in September,1951. I was twenty- three years old and I had been ill for four years, perhaps five, and now I was pronounced cured. I felt supremely healthy and confident, ready to take on the world. But my circumstances at home had changed. I no longer received my thirty shillings through the post. If I wanted money I would have to sign on at the local dole office. Although it was not considered very prestigious to have to sign on, it did not bother me greatly. I went down to the dole office on the first Tuesday after my return. On the way there I fell in with a couple of men with whom I had been to primary school and who had not achieved much with their lives. But they were friendly and sympathetic and gave the impression they felt I had just fallen on hard times and was cut out for something better. I warmed to them.

The dole office was not a pleasant place and by and large the clerks were unpleasant too. When you reported on your twice weekly visit you first had to call out your name. The clerk would then bark out "Any work?" and you would shout back "No work". It was supremely important to the clerk that you made yourself heard otherwise the process would start again. You could not use an Irish name even if it was on your birth certificate: if your name was Seamus you were referred to as James.

Shortly after I had signed on I was offered a job working on the distribution of ration books. There were six of us along with a supervisor. We travelled around in the back of an RUC lorry which was a bit embarrassing for those of us who were Catholics. But it was a nice little job while it lasted and paid well. I knew the man who supervised us. He had a reputation locally for being a great reader and during the lunch break we would talk about books. He had an easygoing attitude to literature and would read anything within reason from Dostoyevski to Frances Parkinson Keyes. He was happy to have found in me a fellow litterateur.

During these two weeks a very strange incident occurred. The ration books were kept in the local RUC barracks, normally a very secure place. One day I was sent to fetch a carton of the books. The normal procedure was to go to the back door and knock and a constable would then let you in. That day the back door was open. I knocked and knocked and there was no reply. So I very gingerly went in. Lying on a long bare table in the middle of the room where the ration books were kept there was a revolver. There was no sound from anywhere. I just picked up a carton and hurried off. I did not mention the revolver to anyone. Chekhov might have made something out of it.

After the job had finished I felt somewhat desolate. I soon realised that the chances of getting a job were very remote. I wrote to big companies and government bodies in Belfast and Dublin without success. My father had an idea that I should write to the Irish Press newspaper group,which was owned by the De Valera family, and explain to them that I was the son of a man who had taken part in the struggle for freedom, but that only elicited a brief reply saying they had no vacancies.

Then I was asked to an interview for an inferior clerical job in the Civil Service in Belfast. I was innocent enough at the time to think I stood a good chance. The pay was around £150 a year, and even the priest who wrote a reference for me wondered if I could live on that. The interview was held in an office in central Belfast. There were eight of us. We each had to go before a panel and be questioned about our suitability. There were about a dozen people round the table: one of them made sympathetic remarks but the others had faces of stone. They concentrated on my experience which of course was non-existent. I soon realised I did not stand a chance. When my interview was over and I waited outside one of the other candidates came over to me. He probably could tell by just looking at me that I was a co-religionist. "Don't worry", he whispered to me. "It's got nothing to do with what you know. Its what you are". The final candidate, well dressed, confident, spoke so loudly we could all hear what he said. He never hesitated for a moment: his words sounded as if they were coming out of a machine. My friend winked at me. Like me he thought it had been all set up. The man came out with a grin on his face. He was followed by a cheery-faced clerk who had a handful of forms. "Sorry, lads", he said to the rest of us. "If you will fill in one of these I'll get you your expenses". My new friend wished me luck. I thought on the way home that of course the man who got the job did give all the right answers. But the old suspicion still lurked.

I hung on a bit longer but I knew then I had little chance of getting work in Ireland. I came to realise that my only option was to return to England so I wrote to Jean and Kevin and they said they would be happy for me to stay with them. When I said goodbye to my parents my father slipped me thirty shillings. I was touched at that. He never had much money and I suppose he realised that a pound wasn't much but could not afford two pounds. In retrospect what made it more touching was the fact that I would never see him again.

This time when I arrived in Farnborough I was in excellent health and feeling very confident. I had made up my mind I would take any job I could find. On the day after I arrived I went down to the local employment exchange. The staff were so much nicer than those in the dole office at home. A kindly woman looked through a card index and found that there was only one job available in Farnborough. A local off-licence wanted an accounts clerk and general assistant. I said I was very interested so she rang up and was told I could go along there and then for an interview. I was offered the job. The pay was not wonderful, about five pounds a week, but I was happy with that. I started work the following day.

The off-licence belonged to a small brewery in South

London which, together with the shop, no longer exists. I did not particularly like the job. Serving in the shop was fine but I was hopeless at the accounts. The manager was a small-minded man with a tendency to be obsequious with wealthy customers. Spirits were in short supply at the time and he liked to produce a bottle, as if he was doing a great favour, and be overwhelmed with thanks.

I enjoyed staying with Jean and Kevin. We often had visitors, usually Irish people from the neighbourhood. Sometimes at weekends, my uncle would come down from London. He had great stories to tell, particularly about his life in the Free State Army during the Civil War. I could never find out why he joined the Free State Army while my father took the Republican side.

On Wednesdays I had the afternoon off and I would frequently go up to London. I loved walking around London, getting a little frisson from seeing places like the Houses of Parliament, Westminster Cathedral and Buckingham Palace. I liked the big stores in Oxford Street and Regent Street and the bookshops in Charing Cross Road. Before I went back I would have something to eat in a Lyons cafe. Even that seemed exciting.

But in October something happened that took my mind off London. We had a telegram saying my father had had an accident and was in the local hospital. For the next few days Jean and I would go down to the phone box and ring up the hospital. He hung on for a few days and then the sister at the hospital told us that he had died. The manager at the off-licence was annoyed when I told him I needed a week off, but I did not give him any option. We got in touch with my uncle in London and he travelled over with us on the ferry.

When we got home my mother was wearing black. She was anxious to tell me about the last days of my father. He had been painting a house on the outskirts of the town and when the owner, a teacher, came home after work she found him lying unconscious outside. He was near a ladder but we never knew whether he had fallen off or not. The death certificate mentioned pneumonia among other causes. He was only sixty-two years old when he died, but I thought of him as a very old man.

He had always been a shadowy figure in my life. I can never remember him holding me or cuddling me. Maybe fathers did not do that in those days. Occasionally he would play with me. Once when I got a little dart board for Christmas we played darts and he showed me how to score. But I never felt he took much interest in my life. Yet after he died my mother told me things that made me realize how much he thought of me. He had boasted to his friends, the men he played snooker with in the evenings, that I had a good job as an accounts clerk and he asked my mother to dig out some of the papers and magazines containing my articles, so that he could show them to some wealthy people for whom he was working. She told me of another time, when I was being assessed for sickness benefit by an official, that he had sat at the top of the stairs by the door listening in case the man should be nasty with me.

I regret that I was not with him at the end so that I could touch his hand and let him know that I cared. My mother and Rita were there. Rita was now married and she and her husband lived in Dublin. It was a fairly modest funeral, but there was a pleasant touch when the members of the local

Gaelic football team, of which he was a staunch supporter, volunteered to carry his coffin to the graveside. There were enough of his relatives to carry out that task, but I know he would have appreciated the gesture.

The funeral service was conducted by an elderly priest, one of the gentlest and kindest of men. Offerings were still being given then and it was now my turn to stand by the priest. When we took the money into the vestry the priest made a very cursory assessment of the amount; he was not interested in money and I think this ritual embarrassed him. Then we carried the coffin down to the open grave where he was laid to rest beside my grandparents.

My father left very little behind in the way of personal possessions: a fairly new suit, his medals and naval discharge book and a few other documents. When I was at Papworth I had sent him a cheap tie at Christmas and apparently he was delighted with it but my mother would not let him wear it: he would have to keep it for special occasions. It was still there wrapped up in cellophane. The old radio sets were all thrown out and my mother was at last able to have one that worked. We gave away the woman's bicycle which had been his only mode of transport for many years. How he ever managed to carry cans of paint and ladders I cannot remember.

It would have been good to have learned about his childhood, his experiences in the Great War and in the fighting in Ireland, and his life in Salford. But he never betrayed the slightest inclination to talk about these matters. I think he had a happy enough life.

After Christmas I started to look seriously for a job in London and was asked to a number of interviews. Eventually I was offered work by a company in Charing Cross Road, which I accepted. It called itself an advertising agency but I soon discovered that this was a rather specious description of the business.

Now I needed to find somewhere to live in London. When I was in hospital the Methodist chaplain told me that if I needed accommodation in London he could arrange for me to stay in a hostel run by his church. But I had also heard about St. Ann's, a Catholic hostel in Stepney, and I arranged to go and visit it. It was in a little cul-de-sac near Brick Lane. All around there was still evidence of bomb damage and the area had a mean impoverished look. By the time I had found the hostel I had little enthusiasm for it. I think Father Ryan, the priest who ran the hotel, was aware of this. He was apologetic about the place. It had once been a convent but the nuns had moved on to somewhere more agreeable. Inside the building was dingy and smelled of stale cooking and sweat. He led me up a stone staircase to where the bedrooms were, little rooms with two single beds. It did not appeal to me very much and he could see that. He told me to think it over and we said goodbye. It was a relief to get away from the area.

The Methodist hostel was in a street off Tottenham Court Road. It was a modern, clean and efficient-looking place. The woman in charge was business-like but not over friendly. I was not asked about my religion and I did not volunteer the information. It was close to where I would work so I decided it would do for the time being.

Needless to say the manager of the off-licence was not pleased when I told him I was leaving. He said he was suspicious because I had been going to London so often, and seemed to imply that there was something underhand about my behaviour. I had no regrets about leaving.

At first the hostel was fine. The little room, a cubicle in fact, was clean and comfortable enough and the food adequate. I could walk to work in a few minutes. Work was the problem. The company's business was the distribution of publicity material. It prepared mailing lists of likely customers and then sent out leaflets and brochures. I was in the section responsible for addressing the envelopes. The more prestigious material was sent in envelopes with typed addresses and this work was done by a number of women in their homes. The less important envelopes were handwritten by a group of pensioners who sat around a table in the basement. My job was to make sure there was a constant supply of envelopes and lists of addresses for both groups.

My immediate superior was a middle-aged woman who took an instant dislike to me. It may have been because she had not been consulted about my appointment or possibly because she did not like Irish people. She always found some little fault in everything I did and she could be very sarcastic. With everyone else she was as nice as pie. Apart from aggravation from this woman it wasn't really much of a job and I soon decided to find something more congenial.

As I was working in the Charing Cross Road and usually spent my lunch hour in the bookshops it occurred to me that bookselling could be a pleasant occupation. I wrote to a number of bookshops asking if they had any vacancies and got a couple of favourable replies asking me to an interview.

One of these was from Collets, which then had two bookshops in Charing Cross Road. I had mixed feelings about Collets which I assumed, though I was never certain, was run by communists. As a Catholic, that placed me in a quandary. But, on the other hand, Collets stocked the publications of the Foreign Languages Publishing House, Moscow, which, in addition to issuing the works of Soviet writers, brought out cheap translations of Russian classics. These were the books that introduced me to Russian literature which I have always loved. I still have a number of them, including a beautifully produced edition of Tolstoy's *Sevastapol*, published in 1946 when Russia would still have been traumatised by the horror and destruction of the war. Also, despite my religion, I maintained for many years a romantic view of the Soviet Union and would regularly buy the illustrated propaganda magazine *Soviet Union* with its ridiculous photographs of heroic Soviet achievements and the boring journal *Soviet Literature* – though it did publish Solzhenitsyn's *One Day in the Life of Ivan Denisovich* in 1963.

I was not entirely happy at the interview with Collets. There was an interviewing panel of three men, pleasant but very earnest. There was mention of joining a union and the pay was poor. Although I was offered a job I just felt that I would always feel a little uneasy working there.

My other interview was with F. & E. Stoneham, a company which had a number of bookshops in the City. I had an old-fashioned gracious meeting with the area manager and a couple of days later received a letter offering me a job in the Old Broad Street shop. I accepted without hesitation. Surprisingly, when I was leaving the advertising agency, my woman supervisor seemed genuinely sorry to see me go.

Bookselling can be an agreeable occupation for anyone prepared to put up with low wages and few prospects of advancement in life. The people who work in bookshops are generally intelligent, easy-going and good-hearted. Those in Stoneham's bookshop were no exception. The manager was a youngish man who preferred to keep a bit aloof. I impressed him soon after my arrival by my knowledge of new books and thereafter we got on well.

There were a number of interesting people working in the shop. One of these was the book collector, a grumpy man of middle European origin. Book collectors are a vanished breed. In the 1950s the large publishing houses had their trade counters in London. When a customer ordered a book the collector would pick it up from the trade counter. He set off early in the morning with his list and returned in the afternoon with a large sack of books. Our collector never seemed to be happy but he knew his way around trade counters. A young man, called John, joined the company soon after me and we became friends. He was Jewish and came from a well-off family but had no ambitions himself. Like me he was very interested in films and in the evenings we would often go together to the cinema. He knew obscure cinemas in the suburbs which showed films that did not make it to the West End. He was not very good in the shop, often turning up late, unshaven and - even worse – without a tie, and was eventually asked to go. I met him again years later working in a little bookshop in Hampstead, little changed. And there was Vicky, a beautiful intelligent young woman with whom I became especially friendly. She was a kind, compassionate and generous person, always helpful to the unfortunate. I suppose I could have pursued our friendship a bit more vigorously, but at the time I never wanted to become too closely involved with anyone.

The one disadvantage of my new job was that I now had to travel to work by underground. But I was also becoming uneasy in the Methodist hostel. Most of those living there were young people who were very keen on their religion. I was constantly being asked to attend prayer meetings. I had the impression that they believed me to be a Methodist and I did not want to disillusion them. So I began to think again about the hostel in Stepney and eventually I got in touch with Father Ryan and asked him if I could move there.

It was a good move. Despite my first impressions, I enjoyed being in St.Ann's hostel. It was a free and easy place. All types of people stayed there. There were many building workers but also a doctor doing postgraduate work at the London Hospital and the commercial attaché at the Jordanian Embassy. For a time I shared a room with a medical student who was reading More's *Utopia*. In the evenings he and I would go out to a weird little café used by Africans and drink coffee.

Stepney, which I had disliked on my first visit, now seemed a fascinating place. All around the hostel were large areas of bomb damage through which I would happily pick my way at night without the slightest fear of being mugged.

There was then a thriving Jewish community and Brick Lane had a synagogue and many Jewish shops. On Sunday mornings, before breakfast, someone would go out to a Jewish bakery and bring in a supply of freshly baked bagels. Sundays brought other delights. The whole surrounding area became a vast market, with people selling all kinds of junk, and on a nice day you could spend hours browsing there. The Thames was a short distance away and could be reached by walking along the Minories and past the Tower of London to London Bridge. Ocean-going ships were then bringing cargo up to the nearby docks. I came to love the whole area.

I continued to contribute to little magazines in Ireland. I must have told the priest about it as he asked me if I could write an article about the hostel for *Christus Rex*, a journal published by St. Patrick's Seminary in Maynooth, which was bringing out a special issue on emigration. I put a lot of work into the article which, when it was eventually published, caused a mild ripple in Irish Catholic circles. It is embarrassing to read it now.

Despite my carefree life, a job that I loved and the good company in the hostel, I was not at ease. I could not get over the feeling that in England I would always be an alien, even though I liked so many things about the place and had no problems fitting into English society. I thought a lot about Ireland, especially Dublin.

After I had been at Stonehams for just over a year it occurred to me that with my experience I might get work in one of the Dublin bookshops, so before I went home on holiday in the summer, I wrote to a number of bookshops there enquiring if they had vacancies. There was a reply from the manager of Browne and Nolan asking me to call when I was in Dublin. A couple of weeks later I was in his office above the shop in Nassau Street. He was a Londoner, who had originally worked for Stoneham's, and knew the manager of the Old Broad Street shop. I was offered a job and a date was fixed for me to start. I walked around the Dublin streets feeling supremely happy. But when I got home and told my mother she did not seem wildly enthusiastic. Perhaps she was shrewder than me about where my future lay.

I got back to the hostel on a Saturday afternoon. People came and went in the hostel and it was not unusual to have a new roommate when you returned from holiday. When I got up to my room there was a fresh-faced young man sitting on one of the beds pulling on his socks. He stood up, gave me a shy smile and held out his hand. He introduced himself in a soft accent as Sean McGahern – he would call himself Sean for a few more years. He told me he was a student at St.Patrick's, Drumcondra, a training college for teachers, and had come over to work on the buildings and earn some money during the summer.

I liked him immediately and believe that he may have found in me a kindred spirit. That evening he was going to a dance and asked me if I would like to go with him but I declined. The thought of trying to dance in one of those lively Irish ballrooms did not appeal. I wish I could remember our conversations. I know we discussed literature a great deal and think at the time he was impressed by my knowledge.

In *Memoir* there is no mention of the hostel yet I believe John stayed there on more than one occasion. He refers to it in the letter he wrote to me before his trip to Europe in 1956. He did not like the place and appears to have had an unhappy encounter with Father Ryan of whom he always spoke disparagingly.

We were not together for long in the hostel. On the Monday I gave in my notice and the following week returned to Ireland. Before I left John and I promised we would meet up again in Dublin.

That chance meeting would have a profound influence on

my life. It was the start of a relationship, sometimes close, that would last for over half-a-century. I did not think then that this gauche country boy would come to be regarded as Ireland's greatest living writer, or that one day my wife and I would crowd into a little country church in Co. Leitrim, together with the great and the humble, for his requiem mass.

SIX

My colleagues at Stoneham's seemed genuinely sorry to see me go and I felt sorry to leave. They were all good and kind people. The shop no longer exists, of course. It was too much to expect a purveyor of culture, however modest, to stand in the way of the advance of mammon. It has been replaced by a towering soulless office building.

As a farewell present I was given a copy of John Harvey's book on Dublin. If I needed convincing that I had made the right decision. Harvey's eulogy to Dublin should have put my mind at ease: "In the whole of Western Europe outside Italy there have, since the fifteenth century, been only three cities with a truly metropolitan stream of culture: Vienna, Paris, London. But Dublin, even if she just misses this rank, comes nearer than any other ...."

Yet, as I crossed over on the ferry, I had an edgy feeling. I had felt safe in England. It was a fair country: bad things could happen there, but there were enough honest and outspoken people to ensure that truth and justice would prevail. I was going to work in the capital of a small, poor country about whose ways I could not be certain.

For the first few months I had lodgings in Drumcondra, not the most exciting area in Dublin. There was one other lodger, a civil servant in his forties, who might have come from the writings of Flann O'Brien. We each had a bedroom and we shared a sitting-room. Our landlady was a pleasant enough woman who would have a few words with us when she brought in meals but otherwise kept out of our way.

Apart from a cinema and a church there was not much else in Drumcondra to relieve the boredom of the place. Is my memory playing tricks or was there really a scale of charges for attending that church? I have this vague recollection that there was a notice on each door stating the amount you were expected to put on the plate as you entered: twopence for the front seas and a penny for those at the back.

Browne and Nolan differed in several respects from Stoneham's. It was a large company with a publishing house and a printing works. Business was conducted with considerable formality. First names were never used. We always addressed one another by our surnames and the appropriate prefix. When the managing director walked through the shop in the morning he raised his hat to the female members of staff. There were seven of us, including myself, in the bookshop plus a cashier who sat in a booth by the door. The cashier had an encyclopaedic knowledge of film stars, especially obscure but significant people like Regis Toomey and Elisha Cooke Junior. I held her in high regard.

There was a large stock of fiction, most of it pretty anodyne because of the strict censorship then in operation. The woman in charge of the fiction section liked to exercise some additional private censorship, withdrawing anything she considered "not our kind of book". There was also a large Catholic section, the responsibility of a quiet little man, near retirement, who would surprise me with occasional outbursts of anti-clericalism.

I shared the non-fiction section with a middle-aged man with interesting acquaintances who would drop in for a chat.

One of these was a teenage boy called Tony O'Reilly, then a student at Blackrock College. Not surprisingly the conversation was about rugby. I had a brief encounter with Tony O'Reilly in the Irish Club in London some years later.. He was then with the Irish Dairy Board and had come to give a lecture. As one of the organisers was about to introduce him to me he quickly held out his hand and said "I know Mr. Whelan". I thought then that this memory for names was the mark of a man who would go far.

I was never sure how comfortable the manager was in his alien surroundings. He had been brought over in hope that his London experience would stimulate business in the bookshop. His appointment may have caused some resentment and I think he gave me the job to provide him with an ally. I got on well with him.

The customers were different from those at Stoneham's. A good proportion were priests and nuns and occasionally a bishop would call. There were celebrities: it was not uncommon for Brendan Behan, Frank O'Connor, or Micheal MacLiammoir to wander in. I had a brief poignant encounter with Jack Yeats, then frail and near the end of his illustrious life. On a rare visit he had picked up a book on Renoir from a metal display stand, which then toppled over causing him some distress. When I – who had been watching with some little wonder – hurried over to help he said "sorry" and I replied that it was all right. Not a momentous event but it has remained in my memory. Once I was asked to take a phone call from Eamon De Valera, who was then the President of the country. He enquired if we could supply two books and for the historical record they were the poems of Thomas Moore and the memoirs of Franz Von Papen. However, I would not want it to be assumed from this that one of the greatest Irishmen of the twentieth century was a lover of sentimental verse or, even worse, an admirer of Nazism. I had to inform him that we had neither book.

At the beginning I was quite happy with my new job. I liked the other members of staff. The pay was very poor but I could still pick up the occasional guinea from my articles and stories. The article I had written about the hostel was published soon after I came to Dublin and was reprinted as the main story in the leading Catholic weekly. That pleased me at the time.

I did not stay in Drumcondra for very long. When the landlady announced that she was putting up the rent I decided to look around for something cheaper and more central. Eventually I moved to a house near Harcourt Street from where it was an easy walk to work. My new landlady was a homely, middle-aged woman with two daughters. It was a three-story house and I had a big room on the top floor where I could have a coal fire in the winter. I ate with the family in the kitchen which was a much more congenial arrangement. The one drawback was the location of the only toilet outside in the yard, a nuisance when you needed to go during the night. But I was happy there and stayed until I left Dublin.

I resumed my friendship with John McGahern and we would meet as frequently as we could. It was not that easy as under the strict regime at St Patrick's – described with some bitter humour in *Memoir* – students were only allowed out on Wednesday afternoons and at weekends.

When we did meet the conversation would invariably turn

to books and writers. Like me, John as a boy had read indiscriminately whatever came to hand – he would always retain a soft spot for Zane Grey – but now he was bent on finding out the truth about great literature.

We both haunted the book stalls on the quays and on my way home from work I might come across him in the little secondhand bookshop in Harcourt Street. It was run by an Englishman, and had an exemplary stock of modern literature at modest prices. I can remember going through the sixpenny stall in the porch along with him and a fellow student. He had picked out a copy of Stevensons's *Weir of Hermiston* and asked my views. I told him that it was said to be one of the best things Stevenson had written, for what that was worth. I never found out what he made of it.

I believe in all modesty that for a time he used me as a kind of mentor, picking my brains not just about books but sometimes more mundane matters. He surprised me once by asking what you did in a restaurant.

It is quite probable that I treated him with a certain condescension – even at times becoming a little irritated by his constant questioning. But maybe a little flattered too. I showed him the article about the hostel with some pride and in general fostered the notion that one day I would achieve great things.

When he qualified he obtained a teaching post in Drogheda and I went down to see him there. We went for a long walk along the bank of the River Boyne. Apart from the quiet beauty of the countryside the place had not much to offer but he expressed his admiration for Drogheda Grammar School, a Quaker institution, and its gifted headmaster, Arnold Marsh. He had booked a table in a restaurant for lunch and was anxious to assure me that it had been recommended by a person of taste. When he moved back to Dublin we saw each other more frequently. I would go over to his room in Clontarf and he would cook a meal of pork chops. I in turn invited him to my lodgings and arranged for my landlady to cook supper for both of us. This genteel arrangement between two young men must seem rather quaint today.

One weekend I invited him to come home with me. My mother was very impressed with his quiet good manners. He came with me to Mass on Sunday. If he had doubts about religion then he did not refer to them. He thought that the outfits worn by the young women seemed drab compared with those seen at his home. I walked him down to the beach and around the harbour and I think he appreciated the beauty of the place.

He never talked much about his own home life. I would have been aware of the death of his mother but I knew nothing about the outlandish behaviour of his father at the time until I read about it in *Memoir*. In fact I knew nothing at all about his family life. After the publication of *The Barracks* I remember referring to his unhappy childhood and he became indignant, insisting that his childhood had been a happy one. So I was not invited to his home for reasons which are now pretty clear. It would be many years before I would visit Leitrim and what would become known as McGahern country.

Over my time in Dublin I observed John grow in confidence and acumen and develop a remarkable insight into literature, notably more so after he enrolled for a BA course at University College. Although he modestly claimed that the degree would help his teaching career I believe he relished the opportunity to debate literature with serious practitioners in the field. So it was not long before our roles were changed and he would gently correct my occasional lapses of taste. At the end I knew there was nothing more I could tell him.

There were many good things about life in Dublin. In particular the theatre enriched my life. I went to see every new production at the Abbey and Gate theatres. The original Abbey building had been burned down by then and the company performed at the Queen's Theatre in Pearse Street. A seat in the gods cost half-a-crown. There I would be in the company of working-class women, some still wearing their pinafores, who clearly enjoyed the performances, particularly of an O'Casey play, and clapped wildly at the end. The Gate, which staged plays by American and European playwrights, attracted a more sophisticated audience. During the intervals it was pleasant to crowd into the little foyer with good-looking well-dressed women.

In fact my enthusiasm for the theatre was so great that I joined an amateur dramatic society, which met in a basement off Parnell Square, and included a number of people who would occasionally act on the professional stage. It was an interesting but not very satisfying experience while it lasted. We rehearsed George Sheil's *Professor Tim*, a not too demanding work and much favoured by amateur groups: it started off well enough but gradually members of the company began to drift away, including the man cast for the leading role. Eventually I was asked to play the lead and when I turned it down the company folded up. Well, I might have made a reasonable job of the part, particularly with my Northern accent, but the thought of making my first appearance in a leading role – even in a parish hall – was just too alarming.

The other great advantage enjoyed by Dublin was its proximity to the seaside. At that time Harcourt Street station was still open and, often in the summer after work, there would still be time to get a train to Killiney. I would have a swim and then lie on the beach and watch the shadow cast by the dying sun move up slowly over the sand and pebbles.

And yet I could never feel entirely at ease in Dublin. Try as I might I could not accept that I shared a common bond with these good, easy-going people whose culture and history I had once felt were also mine. I, too, had grown up in an environment that was nationalist and Catholic, but at the same time there was a certain leaven, not much maybe, from a wider and more secular culture. The city that I had once thought a place of brilliance and charm began to feel terribly dreary. Apart from the theatre, the world of the arts seemed elsewhere. I became increasingly irritated by the sight of so many priests and robed friars striding about with such confident, paternalistic faces, by the arbitrary censorship of books, and by the persistent advocacy of a language that no-one seemed to speak or want to speak To console myself I would listen to the BBC broadcasts on the radio and feel nostalgic about life in England.

There were people who shared my views. John, of course, was one. Another was a young priest who came often into the shop and would discuss with me literature and religion. He was an earnest, enthusiastic man, widely read, who suffered frequently from malaria that he had contracted in South America. He was bored with teaching in a private boys' school and longed to get back to the mission station in the jungle.

And there was a middle-aged Englishman who wrote

detective stories. Marten Cumberland was also a frequent visitor to the bookshop and gradually we struck up a perhaps unlikely friendship. He always wore a smartly cut suit, dark cloth in the winter, light cloth in the summer. At all times he wore a broad-brimmed black hat, then the standard issue for a certain breed of literary man. Marten was born in London in 1892 and had served in the navy in the Great War. In the 1920s and 1930s he had lived in Paris, earning his living from writing for English newspapers. Paris was where he met his wife, Kitty, who, when I knew him, was often in poor health, although she would outlive him. Marten also wrote plays and had had some success in the London stage in the thirties. His comedy *Climbing* was staged at the Phoenix Theatre in 1937 with a cast that included Mary Jerrold, Finlay Currie and O.B. Clarence.

They moved to Dublin at the start of the Second World War so that Kitty would be near her relatives. I don't think Marten ever felt comfortable in an Irish setting but he made the best of it and began a new career as a writer of detective novels. He wrote four books a year, two under his own name and two using the pseudonym Kevin O'Hara. The former were set in Paris and featured a police commissaire called Saturnin Dax, possibly – he would have absolutely denied this – inspired by Simenon's Inspector Maigret. The Kevin O'Brien books relate the exploits of a wise-cracking, London-based private detective. By the time he had given up he would have had over fifty published books to his credit. He made an effort to get involved in the local literary scene and occasionally would have an article published in *The Dublin Magazine*. He also played an active role in the Irish branch of P.E.N. But his heart was really in the London theatre world and he always hoped there would be a revival of his plays.

On Saturdays we would often have afternoon tea in the Royal Hibernian Hotel, and for a couple of hours Martin would reminisce about his life in Paris. He was never boring even though he dominated the conversation. After all, I could never come up with stories such as he could tell of encounters with the likes of Aleister Crowley. He would occasionally take me with him to a matinee in the theatre, especially if there was a show with dancing girls. We would always have a seat near the front. For him it would bring back memories of the cabarets in Paris and I had no objections to watching scantily-clad young women.

When I told Marten of my ambition to be a writer he was full of encouragement, telling me of friends in England who could live well from what in my arrogance I considered hack writing. I had by then given up writing the rubbishy articles and stories and was determined henceforth to concentrate on producing works of literature. Marten was a good and kind friend who tried hard to be of assistance to me at the time and for some years to come.

In 1956 I spent a week in London in interesting circumstances. It was the year when the Angry Young Men were making the headlines. Among the leading figures of the movement was the 24-year old Colin Wilson, whose first book *The Outsider*, described as a study of alienation in the modern world, was published in May and became an immediate best-seller. Few writers can have shot to fame quite so rapidly. Respectable critics were frantically searching for superlatives to describe the work. Cyril Connolly wrote that it was "one of the most remarkable books I have read for a long time" and Dame Edith Sitwell thought the author would be "a truly great writer". A year later, when Colin's second book *Religion and the Rebel* was published, the critics would have a dramatic change of mind.

In the summer of 1956, when he was still firmly on his pedestal, Colin paid a visit to Dublin and came into the shop. I was the only member of staff who recognised him and we had a long conversation. He told me how much he loved Irish writers, Shaw and Joyce in particular. He asked me to come for a drink after work, an invitation I had no hesitation in accepting. Joining us that evening was A.J. Leventhal, known to his friends as "Con", a man of letters and a lecturer in French at Trinity College. I found Con Leventhal, of whom in my ignorance I had never heard, to be a kind, self-effacing man. I knew nothing, of course, of his friendship with Samuel Beckett. In his biography of Beckett, James Knowlson refers to Con Leventhal as Beckett's oldest and dearest friend. I have happy memories of a sunny evening in Dublin enjoying his quiet asides as we listened to Colin's breathless account of his meteoric rise to fame. With us was a young Australian called Hugh, a bit of a drifter with literary pretensions, with whom I would later have a drink from time to time. Maybe he became a great writer.

I can't exactly remember the details of the invitation but, before we parted, Colin told me that if I wanted to visit London he would be happy to provide accommodation. I expect he made the same mistake that we all do from time to time, and assume that this kind of invitation will be treated as a mere formality, never to be taken up. He was not aware of my burning desire to enter the London literary world or that I would regard his casual remark as a means of doing so. I was crass enough to take advantage of his invitation and in

September of that year I went over and spent a week at his flat in Notting Hill. However I was a discreet guest. I went out early in the morning and came back in the evening when there would be a group of visitors, which I was invited to join. There was always animated conversation and I felt I was at the cutting edge of modern thought. When I went into bookshops I had an overwhelming urge to announce: "Guess what, I am staying with Colin Wilson".

When I wrote to thank Colin, he sent me back a long letter apologising for being a poor host and telling me with enthusiasm of the progress of his next book, blissfully unaware of the reception it would receive. To his great credit, he was not defeated by the adverse criticism and over the years went on to produce a vast and diverse range of literature. He did me a service and I am grateful.

That week in London was an exhilerating experience. London seemed a much more vibrant, open, freer place than Dublin. When I returned to work I felt very restless but I hung on for another few months and then I gave in my notice. I had a very small amount of money saved and my intention was to stay at home for a while and try to do some serious writing. John wished me well in my future endeavours and we promised to write. I know now, though he gave no hint then, that he was already embarking on a career that would bring him a fame and adulation he had perhaps never dreamed about. It was pleasant enough at home and I wrote a great deal but not for the last time discarded it all as worthless. After a frustrating couple of months I decided that I needed to find a job and that London was the only obvious destination.

I wrote to the manager of Browne and Nolan to ask if he

could give me a reference and he invited me to visit him at his home in Dalkey. He surprised me by asking me to come back to work for him as assistant manager at a considerably higher salary. It was a beautiful sunny summer day, the manager lived in a handsome house in a very desirable area, and there were implications that if things went well I could have a similar life style. As I sat there I thought about my only other option, returning to the hostel in Stepney and searching for another low-paid job in a bookshop. The manager was very persuasive. He told me he was happy living in Ireland and would never contemplate returning to England. I was flattered, too, that he was so keen to have me working for him. I told him I would accept his offer and I went home dreaming about a comfortable new life, putting aside now any thoughts of London, even of being a writer. I would soon be able to have a nice house by the sea, shared by a warm attractive woman, not startlingly beautiful, just a pleasant intelligent person. We would have children, get to know people and be happy.

The manager said he would sort out the details of my appointment with the company and would write to me at home. The letter came a week later and the news was not good. I could come back but only on the same terms as before and after a time the directors would consider promotion. I wrote back rejecting the offer.

In the late summer of 1956 I returned to the hostel in London where nothing much had changed. I did not want to work again at Stonehams and found a job with the Times Bookshop in Wigmore Street, then probably the most prestigious bookshop in London. I did not like working there: time-keeping was very strict, if you came back from lunch a few minutes late you got a ticking off.

But I acquired some prestige among the staff through my acquaintance with Angus Wilson. It is strange that Angus Wilson is so little regarded today. But when I met him in 1957 he was at the peak of his fame. In the previous year he had published his most famous novel *Anglo-Saxon Attitudes* and other widely acclaimed works were to come. In 1966 he became Chair of English Literature at the University of East Anglia and in 1980 he was knighted.. I had been introduced to Angus by Marten Cumberland. Angus had come over to Dublin for the PEN Congress and Marten, as an officer in the PEN, had taken him to lunch at Jammets where I joined them afterwards for a drink. It would have been interesting to have heard what these two very different men of letters had to say to one another.

Marten had apparently told Angus about my literary ambitions and I was asked to get in touch if I should come to London. I visited Angus at his flat in Dolphin Square a couple of times and each time he took me out for an expensive meal. He would listen with courtesy and patience to my half-baked ideas on literature and offer me advice about writing. Although they were pleasant occasions I was so embarrassed at the cost of the meal that I thought it unfair to call upon his hospitality again. In any case my writing efforts were going so badly, I felt like an imposter.

I acted on one piece of advice he gave me. He thought I should not waste my time working in bookshops but should get a proper job. I came to the conclusion that he was right. At that point in my life looking for a new job was never a problem. The evening papers always had several pages advertising vacancies. But I made a mistake about my first proper job.

I was hired as an accounts clerk by a company that rented telephone systems. Considering my aversion to accounts it puzzles me now why I took the job. The company was in Parker Street, just off Kingsway. I was given a desk in a large office with a dozen other men. A supervisor sat at a desk at the top of the office. Each of us was allocated a number of accounts. My fellow workers were an odd bunch, a few seemed like drop-outs. Most of them were obsessed with sex. They talked a lot about it, sometimes with a degree of wit. If a young woman from another department came in to speak to the supervisor there would be total silence and when she had gone there would be a detailed discussion of her anatomy. It was the only job I have had when at five o'clock there would be a mad rush through the door.

During this period I moved out of the hostel to a bed-sitter in Atkins Road, off Balham High Street. It was a pleasant street of semi-detached houses with little gardens in front, a short walk from Clapham South station. I had a room on the first floor where there were three other men. There was one bathroom between us. I had a bed, a table, an armchair, a wardrobe and a small electric cooker. There was no heating. The landlord, an elderly German and his English wife lived downstairs.

Living in a bedsitter was not easy in the 1950s. There were no supermarkets where you could pick up a cheap lassagna or a shepherds pie on the way home. At Clapham South station there was a small convenience store where I could buy bread and milk and cornish pasties. I would not say I ate too well then.

Whilst I had no close friends I tried to maintain a decent social life. I was helped by Marten Cumberland who put me in touch with his old acquaintances in London. One of these was a man of letters, Rudolfe Louis Megroz – he used the initials R.L. - who enjoyed some fame in his day. His published works included studies of Walter de la Mare, Joseph Conrad and the Sitwells. He invited me to his home in Tufnell Park where he lived with his wife and a vast library of books. He too showed me great kindness. Despite his learning he had the quaint belief that the Catholic Church was involved in a conspiracy to take over the world and to this end was convinced that all writers who were Catholics had a sacred duty to promote their religion in their work.

I became involved with a group of young writers who met weekly at a hall in Victoria under the guidance of the poet and novelist, Laurence Little. The publishers, Hutchinson, had at that time established the Hutchinson Young Authors imprint with the aim of bringing out fiction by new young writers. A couple of those who came to the meeting had books published in this way but, as far as I know, none of them ever achieved fame.

My career as an accounts clerk was fairly short-lived. I quickly realised I was hopeless at the job and decided I would have to find some more congenial work. Across the road from where I worked were the offices of the publishers, Sir Isaac Pitman and Sons ,and seeing it gave me the idea to try for a job in publishing. I spent some time devising a letter of application and wrote to Pitman's and a number of other publishers. Pitman's were the first to reply inviting me to an interview. I was offered a job on the spot as assistant to the publicity manager.

Pitman's are generally associated with shorthand and typewriting manuals but they published a wide range of books on engineering and commerce as well as school textbooks. My main job was writing blurbs and press releases and occasionally designing book jackets and covers. I enjoyed the work and the company of the bright and interesting people with whom I shared an office. My boss, a tall, elegantly- dressed Scot with a distinguished war record, was an easy person to work with. He was a well-known figure in the publishing world and would always take me with him to lunch gatherings of his publishing colleagues.

At one of these the person beside me introduced himself as Reginald Moore. He was pleased that I knew of him as the editor of *Modern Reading*, a paperback series similar to *Penguin New Writing* that came out during the war. Each issue would contain items by Irish writers. He invited me to his home, where I met among others, the writers James Hanley and Muriel Spark. James was very friendly but Muriel eyed me with some suspicion. I would meet up with Reginald occasionally: he was another good man.

John McGahern and I continued to keep in touch by letter. In those early letters he gave no indication that he had any ambition to write fiction. He told me, however, that he had written some poems and agreed to send me copies. I received the poems in July 1958 and in the lengthy letter that accompanied them he expressed his bitterness about his own unsatisfactory life and the depressing condition of his country: "....I do not find life easy: it is very lonely. No-one seems to know about literature anywhere: to realise death......I still teach in Dublin. I often fear that I shall grow old among the primers and children who care as little about learning as I do about teaching.......As long as you believe in yourself nothing can happen to you. Your proper books must be your life, to shape experience, to be able to leave life with some grace".

Of the poems he wrote: "I picked these poems for you from nine or ten that I attempted since Christmas. I have no opinion of them. I could not send them anywhere – I would hate to get them back, you see! I would like to believe that they are not without merit. But it is possible that they have not".

On that occasion he sent me three poems and I have two others that came with later letters. Perhaps they are the only copies that exist.

That summer he spent a few weeks travelling through France and Italy. On his return we met up in London and he gave me a copy of Henry Miller's *Tropic of Cancer* that he had bought in Paris. He was animated about his trip and had acquired a new confidence.

I stayed with Pitman's for a couple of years and for most of the time I enjoyed the work and my life in London. I would write frantically at times, working through reams of paper and slowly forming an idea for a novel. But towards the end of the second year my personal life began to go badly. I became involved in an intense but hopeless love affair with a young woman I had met on the train to Manchester. The circumstances were not particularly romantic. She was doing *The Daily Telegraph* crossword and I volunteered my help. I admit I was then rather naïve about women, maybe still am. She told me she was engaged and on her way to visit her fiance. But we exchanged addresses and we met up again in London and the relationship came to dominate my life.

Then during this tense period I received a letter from John that contained some startling news. He had written a novel and he asked if, as I worked in publishing, I could help him get it published. How can I express this without doing myself an injustice? I regarded him as my friend and I should have been happy for him, but to be truthful I was not cheered up by the letter. It was not quite how I felt things should have turned out. I was the person who was going to write the great book but so far my work had gone nowhere and now my entire life was consumed by a doomed relationship.

But I was also touched,that he should ask my help to get his book published. My problem was that I did not know any of the editorial people in the big publishing houses. I wrote to John asking him to send the manuscript and promising to do the best I could for him. The manuscript was of a work that John soon came to realise was deeply flawed. I felt so myself when I read it but I showed it to the editor of a small general publishing house associated with Pitmans. He too thought it could not be published in its present form. While I was considering how next to proceed I had a letter from John asking me to return the manuscript which he now wished to discard. He told me about the publication of an extract in the journal X and the contract with Faber to write a novel. His life would now be transformed.

Some time in the following year we met up, whether in London or Dublin I cannot recall. John normally behaved with dispassion but on this occasion he was obviously and rightly animated by his dramatic change of fortune. He was eager to tell me about his encounters with his publisher, Faber, and in particular about meeting its director, Thomas Stearns

Eliot. A few years later he would tell me, again with some animation, of attending Eliot's memorial service in Westminster Abbey, where he was seated next to Ezra Pound. I wonder what these two disparate men of letters had to say to one another. I never thought to ask.

John gave me a present of his own well perused copy of *X* containing that fateful extract. I kept it for many years but sadly, during my many changes of residence, it disappeared.

My relationship with Shelagh dragged on making me more depressed. My work at Pitman's was suffering and though my boss was an understanding man there were hints that he was not happy with my behaviour. Eventually Shelagh and I parted with much recrimination. I am sorry, Shelagh, that I had to cause you such unhappiness.

After that I became increasingly lonely and isolated. At weekends I would wander round the local park and look with envy at happy couples and families. I began to tremble at times which worried me so I went to a local doctor and he told me I was suffering from nerves. He prescribed a course of Drinanyl, then popularly know as "purple hearts", which no doctor would casually prescribe today. But they certainly were effective.

I now looked for a means of escape from London and it came in the form of an invitation from Jean to come and stay with them for a while in Manchester. While I was thinking it over there occurred an event which helped me make up my mind. One of my fellow lodgers was a man in his middle fifties, tall, slim, gentle and well-spoken person, with whom I would occasionally exchange a few words. He had a woman friend, a very pleasant person, who would sometimes stay the night contrary to the rules of the establishment. On that account and because his rent was often in arrears, there would often be an exchange of words with the landlord. One day I met the woman friend in the street and she confided that she was worried about her man's depressed state. I sympathised but did not tell her that I didn't feel great myself.

A few days after this meeting when I came back from work I found the landlord beside himself with glee. When he had calmed down he explained that he had just heard that my co-lodger had committed suicide. Apparently he had moved out secretly a couple of days earlier, booked into a nearby hotel, and hanged himself.

The incident was reported in the *Clapham Observer* and I have retained the cutting:

A 58-year old man, registered at a South Side, Clapham Common hotel and was found dead two days later hanging by a cord from a cistern in a lavatory opposite his room, it was stated at a Battersea inquest. He was Desmond Patrick Murray, a steward. Mr. Wilfred Savage, husband of the proprietor of the Courtney Hotel said that Murray booked in at the hotel on Saturday at 7.30 under the name of Russell.

On Monday morning he did not come down to breakfast, so Mr. Savage went up to his room: "Mr. Murray was not in his room. I noticed that the bathroom door was locked, so I knocked on it and said breakfast was ready. When I received no reply I got help and found the deceased hanging from a water pipe by a cord".

Recording a verdict of suicide the Coroner said Murray might well have money problems".

I was disturbed for a long time by the suicide of Desmond Patrick Murray. Surely there could be no worse fate than having to take one's life in the lavatory of a hotel in Clapham Common, South Side. I wondered why he waited until the second morning. Presumably on that first morning he would have had the fried breakfast with coffee and orange juice and have had a word or two with Mrs. Savage. Did he perhaps meet up with his nice woman friend and try to sort things out? I often wondered what happened to her.

I moved to Manchester in 1960 and stayed there for two years, two of the happiest years of my life. I still like Manchester very much but it has lost some of the innocent charm it had fifty odd years ago. So much has gone: the big Lewis department store in Piccadilly with its fantastic sales, the UCP chain of restuarants where you would buy tripe and meat pies. The greatest and most irreplacable loss was the secondhand book market in Shudehill. There were around six stalls selling books at very affordable prices. I remember particularly the shabby old man who came every day with several sacks of books and would gradually empty a sack at a time onto his stall, marking the price on the cover in chalk as he did so.

Jean and Kevin and their three children, Angela, Pat and Gerard, lived in Didsbury, which at the time was a small homely suburb with ordinary little shops and pubs, but is now overflowing with wine bars and expensive dress shops. It was wonderful to be living with a family and to share the innocent pleasures of young children. They were such good-natured children.

I had intended to spend only a short period in Manchester

but I liked the place so much that I decided to look for work. To my surprise I was offered a job by a small publishing company which brought out a number of monthly journals for the engineering and textile trades. I worked in the office of the managing director, who was also the editor of a mechanical engineering journal. My job was to concoct short news items from the press releases sent in by manufacturers and, although I had no knowledge of mechanical engineering, I very quickly became skilful at this task. I also edited and produced a book on spring design, made up of articles that had appeared in the journal, an achievement of which I was very proud.

It was a very easy life. I could have long lunch hours, mostly spent at Shudehill. The managing director smoked a pipe and during the day the office became shrouded in smoke. In the afternoons he would dose off in his chair. Every summer the entire company, twenty or so, would stop work for a day and have an outing by coach. We would visit a stately home or an historic building and then have an excellent meal at a hotel. At Christmas we were taken out to lunch at the restaurant in Kendalls and given a generous bonus. It was a wonderful company to work for. And like all such companies not a trace of it now survives.

When I went home on holiday during my first year in Manchester, I wrote to John and invited him to my home for a weekend. He wrote back offering apologies: "I am desperately trying to build up the shambles, trying to get some order into my working life after all …. I am sure you will understand me working at the same mill. I hope you will write to me soon. I wish you well with your life and work now as always". I don't know why he should have been so dispirited then. He had been given his chance to escape the prison house.

I felt a little flattered at his remark that we were both "working at the same mill". The truth is that I was then writing in earnest. Kevin was studying for a new qualification and every evening he and I would sit down in the same room for a couple of hours and while he studied, I would write non-stop. Towards the end of my second year in Manchester I had completed the first draft of a novel. I was pleased with myself.

My aim now was to work at revising my draft and getting it into shape for sending to a publisher. I had also once more felt the urge to return to Ireland. It seemed a good time to do so. I had a little money saved and could spend some time at home working on the manuscript. I also knew there were new publishing houses in Dublin where, with my four years of experience, I might find a job. And I wanted to get away for one less noble reason. I had broken off a relationship in a heartless way causing some pain to the other person.

I wrote to a number of companies in Dublin describing themselves as publishers and each of them expressed a wish to see me. There was one further reaon to be pleased. The woman who was secretary at the publishing company knew about my literary efforts and volunteered to type up the manuscript without charge. So I set out for home full of hope.

I should have known when I got on the ferry that it would not work out. I felt edgy again as I had in the past. Nonetheless I was still optimistic when I went down to Dublin. I stayed with Rita and Tim and their children, Paul and Mary, for a few days. They now lived in a large and beautiful house overlooking the sea and had offered me accommodation if I found a job in Dublin.

Why is it that my countrymen are so damned considerate, so loath to hurt your feelings by telling you the truth right at the beginning? I had interviews in Dublin with four men who ran small publishing companies: they gave me sherry and would have talked for ages about the state of the country but had no jobs to offer. It would have been so much kinder if they had said so when they wrote to me.

It was disheartening but I was still buoyed up with the thought that I had a novel under my belt. So I went home and began to revise the draft. I sent a couple of chapters to the kind woman in Manchester and they were returned beautifully typed. So far it looked pretty good. I sent another section and that too seemed fine. But then something terrible happened. When I tried to continue I suddenly realised that what I was writing was, once again, unmitigated rubbish. I may have made a mistake in working on the book at home as it was set there during the war years. When I talked to neighbours and walked about the town, seeing the people I grew up with and thinking about their lives, my writing seemed so totally false that I just could not continue. I put away the manuscript and did not look at it again for years.

It was one of the lowest periods in my life and it was to stay that way for a little while. I went to see my old employer in Manchester but he refused to have me back. I know he did so out of kindness. He knew that he would soon be retiring, that the business would close down and that there was no future for me in Manchester. I then realised there was only one avenue open to me. If I wanted to stay in publishing I would have to return to London. Reluctantly I wrote to the hostel in Stepney asking once again if they could put me up and to my old boss at Pitman's asking if there was any prospect of being re-employed there. From both I received positive replies.

I came back to London on a warm Saturday afternoon in late August. It was very depressing getting out at Aldgate East station and walking down Brick Lane: the area was still smelly and squalid. A new priest was running the hostel, a young man less amiable than his predecessor. For that night I was put in a room with three Goan men and a young Londoner. The latter was a friendly sort and both of us went out to a pub in Whitechapel High Street. It was filled with locals. A middle-aged woman, a bit the worse for a drink, came over and propositioned me. It was a very jolly evening. On the way back we stopped and had a Chinese meal. That night I went to bed feeling better than I had for a long time.

On the Monday morning I went along to Pitman's and saw the production manager, a pleasant man about my own age. He had a vacancy for an assistant production manager and he offered me the job. I would stay at Pitmans for the next four years. The situation in the hostel was less good. The showers were open only one day a week and the lavatories were kept in a very poor state. On top of that the place had become infested with bed bugs. But at the time I could not face the prospect of living again in a bed-sitter.

There were always compensations. I was still enormously interested in the cinema and at that time the wonderful magazine *Movie* was being published. It was edited and beautifully designed by Ian Cameron. I have preserved a number of copies but the one I treasure most is issue No. 72

which came out around the time of my return to London. Much of this issue is dedicated to Howard Hawkes but what excited me most was a long review by V.F. Perkins of Samuel Fuller's *Underworld USA*. It begins: "Samuel Fuller's *Underworld USA* has not been given a circuit release. Instead it has appeared, unpublicised at a number of suburban cinemas in a double bill with *I Love, You Love*. Even if there were not a shortage of new films, this would be a waste of one of the best of the year. It is worth travelling to the most sordid and inaccessible cinemas to see it". One of those sordid and inaccessible cinemas was the Gaumont in Brick Lane and I went there on two successive nights to see the film and thought it was great. *Movie* gave arrogant and maybe outrageous reviews of films they believed in, unlike the dull, safe and academic *Sight and Sound*. It always raised my spirits and I owe it a debt of gratitude.

By the following Spring I was desperate to get away from the hostel. I had made one brief foray to a little room in Archway Road but the noise of traffic at night and the loneliness forced me to creep back to Stepney. But then in the summer I had a stroke of luck. In *The New Statesman* there was a little advertisement offering a room in Chelsea to a young man for £1.17s.6d. a week. It seemed too good to be true. But I rang up and was invited to call at an address in Tedworth Square just off the Kings Road. The room was in a flat owned by a middle-aged professional couple who spent the weekends at their house in the country. They lived in the first floor and let out the two basement rooms, one of which was vacant. I don't think they needed the money but they wanted to have someone living in the flat when they were away. They liked me and offered me the room which I took without any hesitation. The situation could not have been more desirable, a room just off the glittering Kings Road in the 1960s. The other tenant was a man a couple of years older than me who worked for the TUC. Denis and I quickly became good friends.

Though I soon felt at ease in my new accommodation and with my new companion I took precautions to make sure I would not again suffer from loneliness. I had already joined a number of cultural organisations and became a member of the Irish Club in Eaton Square. Denis and I would go there for a drink and the good company several evenings a week. Life was feeling very good once more.

During 1963 John's first novel *The Barracks* was published and the literary world in Ireland and Britain quickly recognised the appearance of a writer of enormous talent. Reviewer after reviewer heaped praise upon the book. I still have my copy of the first edition, with its plain dust wrapper, and on the back flap the photograph of a young country boy, looking as if he had just been spruced up for his Confirmation.

During the summer we met in London. I had already written to him when the book appeared to offer my congratulations and now there was nothing more I could offer in the way of praise that would have been meaningful. He had received the accolades of those who mattered in that new world to which he had gained entry. He was, however, concerned about the physical appearance of the book and sought my assurance that the production was of a high standard.

Later that year I met him again in Dublin. We went for a drink in the Brazen Head pub which he thought would be free from literary poseurs and he asked if I would like to go to a party that evening given by an academic friend. For a gathering of literary people and their hangers-on it was a pretty lively evening. John introduced me to Francis Stuart, who had become something of a legendary figure. His gentle old fashioned courteous manner seemed to belie a turbulent and controversial past.

I managed to get drunk and had a dispute with Benedict Kiely, but it was a great evening. When I got back to London I had a letter from John saying he hoped I had enjoyed the party as he had felt I might have been depressed or bored. He wrote: "I finished the first rough draft of the novel, but got ill, and I'm not supposed to work for some time. But I'm sick of here, I want to go, but the work is far too important to me to risk it in change, but I wish it was done".

Early in 1964 he was awarded the Macauley Travelling Fellowship for what was then the large sum of £1000. When I again sent my congratulations he wrote back to thank me: "I'll go away, but I'm finishing the novel first, and I haven't thought about it in any real way. It's nearly finished but it almost killed me. .... I read a few marvellous savage stories by Gogol and Metamorphosis by Kafka which I thought extraordinarily accurate, but not much else. I hope you have a nice Easter I'd be grateful if you remembered me to your mother very much. I wouldn't mind going home for a few days just to look at the woods and river .....but there's no use grumbling..........".

Over the next year or so we would regularly meet in London. Once we went to Regent's Park and hired a boat and he showed me the correct way to row. *The Dark* was published in 1965 and was quickly banned in Ireland. Just before he returned to Dublin we went for a drink to Dirty Dick's in Bishopsgate and he told me what he thought could await him on his return to school. He said that while he had no particular wish to go back to teaching he was keen to face up to his superiors. He also told me about his marriage to Anniki Laski and of the time they had spent in Finland and in Leningrad meeting with Russian litterati.

The story of his treatment by the establishments both clerical and lay has been told many times. He gave me a first-hand account on his return to London. It was told in a light-hearted way but I think it affected him more deeply than he cared to admit at the time. On another occasion I met up with both him and Anniki, who was a very good-looking young woman. We had lunch and went to a film at the Academy Cinema in Oxford Street. Afterwards they quarrelled over some trivial matter and I felt that their relationship was not entirely happy.

Meanwhile my own life went on serenely enough but from time to time I would sit back and take stock. In 1966 I was thirty-eight years old. I had a pleasant but not very well-paid job and lived in a very agreeable area of London. Every summer I went back to Ireland for two weeks, always spending a few days in Dublin. Only once did I experience foreign travel when I went with an acquaintance on a short visit to Venice and Paris. I had failed to become a creative writer. It was not a lot to have achieved halfway through my working life.

I kept a constant lookout for a more lucrative job. But at the time publishing was changing and gradually ceasing to be an occupation for gentlemen. There were not many companies like Pitman's left. Then in May of 1966 I saw an advertisement for a post of publications officer at Northampton Polytechnic. I had never heard of Northampton Polytechnic, which was not apparently in Northampton but in Islington. Later that year along with the other polytechnics it was to become a university. Its new name would be City University.

I applied for the job and was asked for an interview. The interview was held in the institution's main building, an uninspiring example of Victorian architecture situated among high rise blocks of council flats in a rather depressing area. I was interviewed by the registrar and an assistant registrar. They wanted someone to be responsible for producing the many prospectuses and brochures which the new university anticipated it would require. I felt they were impressed by my qualifications. Among the documents the registrar had in front of him I spotted a long letter in the handwriting of my old boss in Manchester, I was sure would have given me a good endorsement. I went away feeling very hopeful.

At around this time I came upon an advertisement for a job on a technical magazine in Dublin which impulsively I applied for. During the following week when I was at home on holiday I went to see the editor. I was offered the job which paid well but I was not entirely happy with the editor. He had a photograph of the late President Kennedy on his desk. I have nothing against President Kennedy but I am suspicious of people who have photographs of him on their desks. I agreed to think the matter over.

Then the letter came from London offering me the job at the university and I knew it was what I wanted: I wrote back accepting the offer. My mother, although she would dearly have loved me to stay near her, told me that I had done the right thing. "You were always happier over there" she said.

I started working at City University in September and, although there were periods of trial, I would remain there until I retired twenty-eight years later. And during that first somewhat confusing week I met the young woman who would become my wife.

SEVEN

Before this I had from time to time given some thought to my future life and had accepted that I would probably remain a bachelor and a celebate one at that. It might not be so bad. I had grown up in a culture where a virtuous single life was thought commendable.

Yet I loved the company of women and in gatherings would prefer to converse with them. They always seemed more interesting than men. They were understanding and sympathetic and did not rejoice at the misfortunes of others. They rarely wanted to discuss football or cricket – tennis maybe – and could not tell how many miles to the gallon their cars could achieve – or for that matter care. They were also often beautiful and desirable.

There were a number of women with whom I would go out for a meal or to the cinema or a concert. One of these I believe cared for me: she was a good and kind person, probably too good and kind, and I might have saved her from a future of loneliness and penury. But I could not conceive having a lifelong relationship with any of them.

While it seemed a bleak enough outlook I did not let the prospect weigh me down. There were so many things to do in London. I never felt lonely. On the evenings that I did not go to the Irish Club there was always a new play to see or friends to visit or some other event to attend.

On Saturdays I could easily spend all day going around secondhand bookshops and I had acquired a new interest, classical music. Denis had an expensive record player and a collection of classical recordings and hearing these made me realise it was time to move beyond Ravel's *Bolero*. So I bought my own less sophisticated record player and began to browse in record shops. I was a bit nervous in record shops at first as there always seemed to be people there with an astonishing knowledge of music and prepared to spend large sums of money on records. I was quite happy with the inexpensive records brought out by Classics for Pleasure and Camden Classics. To be honest, I could never really get to the bottom of classical music myself and had to take the reviewers' judgements on trust.

Occasionally I would conjure up visions of what my life might be like when I got old. There seemed to be two possibilities. One was a little flat in London from where I could still go to the cinema, do the rounds of the secondhand bookshops, meet up with old friends and from time to time have people round for a meal: something simple like a roast which I would carve on the table, accompanied by a bottle or two of decent wine with maybe some Mozart playing in the background. I would get to know the people in the other flats and hope that, when I got really old and immobile, some kind young couple would take an interest in me, maybe do my shopping and bring me in a hot meal. At other times I thought I might go back to where I came from, find a cottage near the sea and hope that there would still be some old childhood companions with whom I could reminisce. And, if I was near enough to the church, I could go to Mass on weekday mornings with people old like myself and who, like me, were making sure of their place in the world to come. On the odd day I would get the bus to Belfast and browse around Smithfield and have a lunch of lamb chops and cabbage and boiled potatoes. I might even go to Dublin for a couple of nights and maybe see a play at the Abbey.

Neither of these options seemed too bad and I could go about my life without too much care for the future. And then it all changed. When I met Mary, probably that very first time, I knew beyond any doubt that my future life would inevitably be linked with hers. I do not understand why this should have been so. She was several years younger than me, extrovert, liked dancing and parties. She was born in Plumpton in Sussex, that most English of counties, and baptised and confirmed in the Church of England. Her father was a policeman and they moved to Seaford, a small town on the south Coast near to Brighton. That was where she spent her teenage years, going to Lewes Grammar School, an experience she enjoyed a great deal more than I enjoyed my time at the Abbey school. Seaford is not the most exciting of seaside towns, but it has a homely charm. Some day we might go and live there.

Naturally she did not know a great deal about my country or my religion but she was quick to acquire a working knowledge of both matters, though even now things will come to light that will cause her consternation. Despite such disparities we came to discover that we had so much in common, a left-wing view of politics, a dislike of privilege and pretense and a happy ability to often enjoy the same books, plays, films – sometimes even the same jokes.

Until then I had very little experience of English family life. Even when I was with Jean and Kevin in Manchester, our closest friends were generally other Irish families. Now I became involved with a network of English people, many of whom lived in rural Sussex. Without exception they were kind and hospitable and welcomed me warmly into their homes. Most of the older people that I met have now passed on but I have fond memories of them.

I met Mary her father had just retired from the police and he and his wife had moved to Heathfield, a pleasant village about 20 miles from the coast. We would often go there at the weekend. From there we could visit Hastings, Eastbourne, and Lewes. Mary's father would take us for drives into the Sussex countryside, which has a beauty different from, but no less wonderful than, that of the countryside of my childhood. We both loved those weekends in the country and hated having to return to London on Sunday evening. I expect Mary's parents would have been alarmed at the prospect of their daughter's liaison with an Irishman of mature years. But if they were they kept their feelings from me. They were a warm and generous couple and I quickly came to love them.

With the advent of Mary there also came a new circle of friends in London. She lived in a flat in Harley Street with four other girls all jolly, witty and friendly. I would go there frequently to enjoy their good-humoured banter and to listen to tales of their romances. Life had become very good for me.

Of course I knew that we would inevitably get married but I was quite happy to carry on with as much of my old way of life as possible and did not see any necessity for fixing a wedding date in the immediate future. But that was not – I would come to realize – how Mary saw the matter.

While my social life was becoming ever more agreeable I was less than enchanted by my new job at the University. I had joined the staff there at the time of its transition from humble polytechnic to the exalted status of university. There were not many universities then and they still had a certain aura of grandeur and mystery. Certainly the authorities at the new City University had no intention of dispelling that aura. New people from the older universities, who knew about such matters, were appointed to the administration and much of their time, energy and brain power was being devoted to the task of adapting the institution to its new role.

My immediate superior was a sensible man, who had served the polytechnic in a senior role for many years, and whom I suspect saw no great need for change and was probably embarrassed, perhaps even saddened, at the sight of well-educated men and women deploying their considerable intellects on devising the rituals and other trivia without which a centre for higher education could not flourish. All he could offer me in the way of work was proof-reading the prospectus then a mean-looking little booklet, the work of a local printer. He tried to lift my spirits with the assurance that there would an abundance of publications once the university got into its stride. But it seemed a poor prospect when I considered the many books I had helped to produce and my dealings with leading printers and bookbinders and paper merchants, who would court my business. And it did not help either to discover that someone else from the publishing world had been appointed – at a much higher salary than me

– to take charge of the University's publicity and who would have encroached into my territory if I had not warned him off. We got on all right after that.

Before I started the job I suppose I had a naïve idea of what working in a university – even a small and new university – would be like. I had envisaged intellectual debate – perhaps above my comprehension, dry humour, graciousness. When I was in publishing the people I worked with were lively, well informed about politics and the arts, liberal in their views. To my dismay I found in those early days that many of my new colleagues were quite the opposite, conservative both in outlook and attire and a little philistine.

Courses in engineering and applied science predominated and the vice-chancellor, a kindly paternalistic man, considered the main function of the institution was to train young men – possibly young women – for careers in industry. Consequently in the common room the merits of the latest car designs were more likely to be discussed than the latest play by Harold Pinter. As a concession to the wider academic world, there was a small social science department where lecturers dressed less formally and were familiar with the writings of strange and suspect characters like Emile Durkheim and Max Weber. Among themselves the other staff would snigger at the work of this department as more orthodox Christians might do at the beliefs of the Jehovah's Witnesses.

In fact, the really lively and interesting people at that time were the young women in secretarial jobs like Mary. She came to the University soon after me and for a time worked in an adjacent office. She was funny and irreverent and knew what was going on in the world. An exchange of good-natured banter with her would cheer up my day.

After a few weeks at the university I felt I had made a serious mistake. I missed being with people who understood type sizes and the weights of paper and the strengths and weaknesses of printers, mundane though these skills might be. I wrote to a number of publishers explaining my predicament but nothing of interest turned up. Yet as time went by and despite all the frustrations, I began to form an attachment – always tenuous to the institution that would nurture me for more than a quarter of a century.

Whatever my reservations about the university, I liked its neighbourhood from the beginning. In the 1960s Islington seemed very down-at-heel but it was also surprisingly attractive. The University's main entrance was then in St. John Street and walking up from there to the Angel underground station you would pass a couple of good pubs, a secondhand bookshop, a butcher, a greengrocer, a fish-and-chip shop and an inexpensive Italian restaurant Past the Angel were the antique shops and stalls in Campden Passage and Chapel Market where I would buy much of the fruit for our family. I think most of that is now gone and you would be hard put to get a cup of tea and a sandwich in the area. The wine bar and the expense account restaurant have taken over.

One unique attraction in the area would survive throughout my time there: George Jeffery's bookstalls in Farringdon Road, a wide, busy and faceless street that runs from Kings Cross down to Holborn Viaduct. Once there was a flourishing book market along Farringdon Road and George Jeffery, who took over from his father in 1957, was the last of the stall holders. He had four or five stalls which opened on Saturday mornings and at lunch-time during the week.

On Saturday mornings there was a sale of newly acquired stock and the stalls would be surrounded by dealers waiting to pounce once the covers had been removed. Bookdealers, contrary to popular perception, can be nasty aggressive people and it was not pleasant there on Saturdays.

But on weekdays, in addition to his regular stock, George provided a little treat for a loyal band of customers, of whom I was one, who patronised him winter and summer, year in and out. Each day after he had uncovered his stalls George would take from the back of his van several sackloads of books which he would empty onto the pavement. These would be priced at half-a-crown or less and among them it was not uncommon to find a valuable first edition. We watched with bated breath but could not move until he had emptied all the sacks and given us the nod. We grovelled then on the pavement like starving men who had been tossed a few crusts. Passers-by would stare at this strange spectacle. George looked on with a grin.

We were indeed a strange bunch, mostly middle-aged men. I can recall only one woman, an American lady who wrote detective stories. The others would be difficult to pin down. Among the regulars were two elderly men, well dressed, respectable, from the accents middle-European in origin. One day they fought physically over possession of a book and George had to step in and separate them. But Harry was the person I remember most. A tall and slightly shabby man, very well spoken and intelligent, he came every day on an ancient bicycle. He knew I was interested in Irish books and would pass on to me any he found. He was always getting into trouble with George because he would put aside books which he then did not buy. Probably could not afford to. I cannot imagine how Harry survived when George eventually closed down.

Although I visited his stalls for a quarter of a century I never became remotely friendly with George. One or two of the regulars did converse with him but I always felt there was a degree of sufferance on the part of George. I was not around when the stalls were covered up for the last time in the early 1990s. I saw him once after that as he was coming out of the bookshop that his son had opened in Clerkenwell Road. He gave me a friendly smile of recognition and we exchanged a few words. He died soon afterwards.

Soon after meeting Mary I told her about my ambition to be a writer and of my unhappy experience with the novel I had abandoned. She encouraged me to resurrect it and offered to type it for me at the weekends, using the little Remington typewriter I owned. I had bought the typewriter when I still believed I could be a writer but had never learned to type. Mary was very good at giving encouragement and still is. So I set about revising the manuscript removing what I thought were the more outlandish elements in the plot and Mary dutifully typed it for me. At the beginning I had some enthusiasm. I knew it might not make a masterpiece but it could become a modest narrative of boyhood in Northern Ireland. I would happily settle for that.

John McGahern was now working in London as a supply teacher and I would still meet up with him for a drink. Since the publication of *The Dark* his reputation had grown dramatically in Ireland and he was now highly regarded in literary circles in Britain. His honest portrayal of life in a remote part of rural Ireland, free from sentimentality and sensation, would never appeal greatly to the general reader in Britain, who if they read about Ireland at all, preferred stories of whimsical romance or of squalor and degradation.

John had by now acquired a considerable gravitas as well as a vast knowledge of literature which I must confess impressed me. He was not slow to pronounce, often unfavourably, on any author whose name cropped up in our conversations. I did not always agree with him but I liked his sweeping dogmatic judgements. When my work was getting near completion I mentioned it to him and asked if he would read it and give me his views. He did not show any great surprise and we arranged to meet again at our usual rendezvous, Dirty Dick's.

I was very nervous as I waited for the last few pages to be typed. Some years earlier, I had shown a section of the original manuscript to R.L. Megroz and he had praised the writing while considering the content to be depressing. "Why do the Irish always feel sorry for themselves?" he asked. A judgement as benign as that would please me well enough but I feared the worst. The manuscript was in an envelope and when I handed it to John he felt the weight. He asked me how many words there were, and I said forty five thousand. He shook his head: "It's a bit short. That will make them suspicious". When we had finished our drinks he went off with the package under his arm.

The next evening he rang me up. He told me what I already really knew. It was no good. He was as kind as possible in the circumstances like a doctor explaining to a patient he has incurable cancer. He told me there were some good things, in particular a section set on the beach in summer, which *was* pretty good. But there were some episodes that were just not credible. That also was true. However he explained that the main problem was that I was not in control of the material. He sounded embarrassed and I felt sorry about the whole situation. We agreed to meet so that we could have a more detailed discussion. But a couple of days later the manuscript arrived in the post. There was a short note: "Dear Tony, I am sorry about the conversation on the telephone. I still feel the work falls into some limbo. Rather than ring you I think its better to post it and if, when you think of it, I can be of any use I'll be grateful and glad. John". Of course I felt upset, even though I agreed entirely with his judgement. I was upset for a very long time. Mary thought I should ignore John's views and send the manuscript to a publisher but I was not prepared to do that. I put it away and did not look at it again.

I was in a strange situation. For a brief moment it had seemed possible that I might again enter into the company of creative artists but I now knew that it would not be possible. In Hardy's *A Pair of Blue Eyes*, the dilettante Henry Knight discusses with his lover, Elfrige, his inability to write a novel: "Anybody's life may be just as romantic and strange and interesting if he or she fails as if he or she succeeds. All the difference is, that the last chapter is wanting in the story". I felt like that. I could not write the last chapter.

I did not see or hear from John for a quarter of a century, until indeed we were both beginning to feel old. I just could not think of a good reason to get in touch. I never knew and now never will know what, if anything, he felt about me at the time or whether he understood why it would be difficult for me to get in touch. For my part, I was probably waiting until

I had at last written something of which I could be proud and of which I could ignore any criticism. But I did not try to write again, not for very many years.

Of course, I followed his career. I read reviews and articles about him and Rita would send me cuttings from Irish newspapers which I kept in a folder. I always tried to convey his virtues to my English friends, intelligent people who endeavoured to keep abreast of modern literture and yet shied away from a great Irish writer's uncompromising portrayal of rural life. Whenever I was in France I would go into bookshops to check if there were French editions of his work on the shelves. He was always an enormous presence in my life.

I was a very tardy suitor. After three years there was no sign of a proposal from me so, in an effort to test my sincerity, Mary went back-packing with a friend across Spain and Morocco for a few months. When she had gone I quickly became aware of how much a part of my life she had become. I would go down to see her parents from time to time, but it was no longer such an enjoyable experience.

During Mary's absence the so-called "Troubles" broke out in Northern Ireland. In the weeks before, although I was remote from it all, I could sense that some terrible calamity was looming. I have kept a cutting from *The Times* for 9th August 1969 of a report from Derry on the tense situation before the catalystic Orange parade. It quotes Eddie McAteer, the leader of the old Nationalist Party, as foreseeing a conflict that could "raise the curtain on the last terrible act of the age-old Irish drama". Eddie and the Nationalist Party have long passed into history, but I have often thought of the truth of those words. For many years to come Northern Ireland would be prominent among my thoughts, often with sadness but occasionally with a little hope. Mary, too, would become familiar with names like Faulkner, Hume, Adams and Paisley.

Soon after she returned from her travels we fixed a date for the wedding and in the following April, we were married in the little Catholic church in Heathfield. I feel sorry now that Mary could not have been married in her own parish church, but I knew at the time that such a marriage would not have been recognised as valid by my own church, which was a very sad and unnecessary state of affairs. We had a honeymoon in Paris and then lived for a year in a flat in Muswell Hill.

During that year Mary came with me to Ireland on her first visit. I wasn't sure how she would react, but I need not have worried as she loved the place from the start. We had no car then and we travelled on the overnight ferry from Liverpool to Dublin and then took the train to Galway, where we had booked accommodation for a few days. I myself had not seen much of Ireland, apart from Belfast and Dublin, and so we both experienced for the first time the landscape of the Western seaboard. We went on a bus tour of Connemara and took the ferry from Galway to Inis Mor, the largest of the Aran Islands, where we walked to the great fort of Dun Aengus. The West of Ireland was a happy choice for that first visit. We both loved the area and have been back many times since.

From Galway we went back to Dublin, and stayed for a few days with Rita and her husband Tim, exploring a little of that charming city that had in the past both seduced and later repelled me. Then we headed North to visit my mother and to show Mary that very different but still very beautiful land where I had spent my boyhood. Mary can be a very outspoken person and I tried as best I could to impress on her the need to guard her tongue in that part of the world. Tim drove us to Kilkeel. The troubles had not long begun and had yet to reach their full ferocity, but we still felt a little frisson of excitement as we went through the border checkpoint. Once past Newry we followed the beautiful shoreline of Carlingford Lough and then, at Rostrevor, Tim took a detour that would bring us through the Mourne Mountains. It was an impressive journey.

We spent two weeks with my mother during which we walked out to see the cottage, down to the beach and round the harbour and called in on people I knew in the town. We both enjoyed the holiday and I was glad – and relieved – that Mary had liked Ireland.

Property was pretty cheap in London at the time and we could have bought a nice house in Muswell Hill for eight or nine thousand pounds. But we both felt we had our fill of London and, while we were content to work there, we wanted to do our living in a less frantic setting. We eventually bought a house in Tonbridge, an unpretentious town in Kent thirty miles South of London with excellent train connections to the capital. The house had a large garden in which I grew vegetables and Mary cultivated flowers. Mary's father, an experienced gardener, was always ready with advice. I learned the skills of decorating and elementary carpentry and the other tasks that are expected of a male house owner. At first Mary and I commuted to London but Mary then obtained a job with the local social services department working with the blind and partially sighted. It was a job she loved.

She gave up work for a time when we adopted two children, a brother and sister, Amanda and Gunter, whose coming greatly enriched our lives and those of their new extended family. At first my mother had expressed reservations about our adopting children but when we brought them over to meet her she quickly grew very fond of them. I think they enjoyed that visit which gave them a sense of attachment to Ireland. They would make many more visits there over the years.

Despite the occasional traumas that occur as children grow up our lives were now remarkably tranquil. We made some new friends and kept many of the old ones. We went for excursions to the seaside and into the country. The highlight of every year was the camping holiday in France, at the beginning by the Mediteranean and later on the West coast. It involved some hard work. There was the chore of loading the car the day before, the tiring two-day drive to the campsite, and then the exasperating task of erecting our big frame tent. Yet, looking back, I think that for me those camping holidays were periods of inordinate happiness.

During the year my mother would move between the houses of my sisters and there would also be a visit to us in Tonbridge. She would always visit Mary's parents with whom she had formed a close attachment. Then in the summer she would return home to await the arrival of her children and grandchildren. Over the years the character of our little street began to change. The old families either died off or went elsewhere and the young people who moved in were not content with an outside lavatory or the lack of a proper kitchen and bathroom. So extensions were built on, containing all the necessities for modern living. But our house was left behind. I don't think my mother cared very much at first. She liked her basement kitchen where she would sit reading late into the night before going up three flights of stairs to her bed in the attic. But, when she became very old, she began to feel envious of the luxuriously fitted out houses of her neighbours and it was difficult to know how she could be helped without a large expenditure, which at the time none of us could afford. My sister Jean, had bought a little cottage just outside the town which had a bathroom and a fitted kitchen, and to which my mother could have moved. But she was reluctant to leave the little street in the middle of the town. In the end it did not matter too much. She became very frail and unable to continue her travels. A home help came every day, a good, kind young woman of whom she became very fond.

In the summer of 1980, not long before she died, I decided to go over over on my own and spend a week with her. It was a very happy period. She was overjoyed that I had come but it was sad for me to see how thin and wasted she had become. During the week I did the cooking on the stove in the kitchen. She was never really happy with that stove. When we first moved into the house she had a new coal-burning stove installed. It had everything she required of a stove: an oven for roasting, a top for frying and griddling and boiling water, a grill in front for toast. It also gave out a great heat, warming the whole house. The first thing every morning she would light the stove and keep it going all day, winter and summer. But eventually the stove wore out and it was difficult to get a replacement. When we were over we had to take her around all the hardware stores to look for a stove. But that kind of multipurpose stove had gone out of fashion then. Eventually she got a secondhand stove from a house that was being refurbished but of course it was never as good as the original one. But it did me all right during that week.

I cooked one memorable meal. A neighbour who was a

fisherman, left us in some herrings and I fried them on the stove. Herrings were a staple diet when I was growing up and, going past any Catholic house on a Friday, you could smell herrings being fried. I loved fried herrings but, on the few occasions when I got them in England, they seemed soggy and tasteless. Anyhow I put the frying pan on the stove and chucked in the herrings with a bit of fat and soon they were sizzling. From time to time my mother would get up out of her chair to see how they were doing. At last I thought they must be done. The had turned a nice brown colour. But my mother had a look and said "No, a wee bit more". She finally accepted that they were cooked and we sat down and ate two herrings each with boiled potatoes. You must take my word for it that they were delicious: crispy on the outside and soft and dry on the inside. And there are people who will tell you that you only need to cook fish for a minute or two.

My mother was not interested in much now. I bought her the Daily Mail, which she had always liked even though its politics were not hers, but she barely glanced at it. On Sunday she was no longer able to get to Mass. She had not been for ages so I set out to walk there and along the way got a lift from my old friend Cecil. He himself would be dead within a few years. It was strange being in the church without my mother.

That afternoon Tim unexpectedly turned up and we went out for a drive. We drove past the top of the lane where the cottage was but she did not want to see it. We stopped at a couple of houses where she was known and the people came out to have a word with her. Then we went on to Greencastle from where she and her brothers had, many years before, crossed over to Greenore to take the ferry to Liverpool and then the steamer to New York. She got out of the car and went over to look across the lough. I have a photograph of her as she stood there, a wistful expression on he wasted face.

Later we visited Leonard and Margaret, two old friends who had once lived down the street from us and with whom we had maintained a warm relationship over many years. Leonard was an Orangeman, in fact a member of The Royal Black Preceptory. I can still see my mother sitting down in their house that Sunday talking happily with the pair of them. "I never go to church now": she announced. "No matter" Leonard said. "You went when you could. Not like some of them".

One day she suddenly asked me if I thought there really was a life after death and I assured her there was, which I think put her mind at ease. I was touched by this incident and at the time thought it strange that someone who had believed all her life should still ask for reassurance. But, now that I too am old, I better understand her need.

When we kissed goodbye on the last morning I sensed that I would not do so ever again. I can still feel that aged tear-stained face against mine. The kind woman who was her home help drove me to the airport. Our next door neighbour, a young woman who too had been good to my mother, came with us. It was comforting to know that with such people around she would not be neglected.

She carried on in the house for a few weeks and eventually moved into a care home, which had recently been opened. After a few days there she contracted pneumonia and was transferred to the local hospital. When I heard she was in hospital I rang up every day but it was never made clear to me how much time she had left. On the morning of the day she died the sister in the hospital told me I had better come over quickly. I got a flight to Belfast but it was too late. Both my sisters were with her when she died and I still feel bad that I was not there too. I suppose I had got into the English way of thinking that work was so important.

According to local custom the funeral would be on the following day and my immediate task was to see the undertaker. Like many Irish undertakers then – and probably quite a few still – he was a publican and he gave me a large glass of whiskey as we discussed the arrangements in the bar. In the early evening my mother's remains were taken from the hospital mortuary to the church. A small number of people would accompany them and we had hired a couple of cars. When we drove up to the hospital the undertaker was there with the hearse. One of the curates was also there along with a few friends and neighbours, including Leonard and Margaret. We went into the little mortuary and I asked the undertaker if he would open the coffin so that I could have one last look at my mother. She looked very small and peaceful. I bent down and kissed her on the forehead. The priest said the *Our Father* and we all joined in. I was glad he did not say some specifically Catholic prayers which might have embarrassed Leonard and Margaret.

Then the coffin was closed and we set out to carry it a little way down the hospital avenue. I asked Leonard if he would like to help carry it and he said he would. So together with Tim and some friends we carried it down the avenue on our shoulders before placing it in the hearse. We then drove slowly to the church where the coffin was placed on a catafalque before the altar and there was a short service. Leonard and Margaret sat at the back of the church. I should point out that Orangemen, then at least, were forbidden to enter Catholic churches so Leonard was breaking the rules out of his regard for my mother. He is dead now and I doubt if that lapse would have caused him difficulties at the heavenly gates.

There was a large crowd at the requiem mass the next day. It was celebrated by one of the priests who had been at the college in Farnborough and now worked in Belfast. Jean had kept in touch with him. He had read the death notice in *The Irish News* and had come down that morning. It was a nice arrangement and one that my mother would have loved. She was not always a great admirer of priests but would have been pleased that one had made a special journey to celebrate her requiem mass.

Afterwards we carried her coffin down to the family grave and laid her down beside my father and her parents. There could be few better places than this to rest until the judgement day, beside the church she attended as a child and throughout most of her life with the beautiful mountains rising up behind. I thought of all those Sunday mornings when, whatever the weather, she would get up to catch the bus to the church for half -eight mass and afterwards would hurry down through the graveyard to say a prayer at this grave. She always took great pride in the grave. The original plot was only half the size but she bought an extra piece so that there would be room for the rest of us.

I stayed on for a few days, more sorting out my mother's affairs and registering her death. Each of us took back some of my mother's little store of treasures. I carried away the *Cyclopedia of Ireland*, a beautiful oil lamp, two brass candlesticks and one of the ornamental aeroplanes. It was hard to believe that someone you had loved so much had gone for ever. She still seems very close to me.

Not long after my mother's death we moved to a new house in Tonbridge. It was a large, three storeyed house in a pleasant street within walking distance of the railway station. At the time the purchase stretched our financial resources to the limit but we survived. It required decorating throughout which we did ourselves with the help of Mary's father. I perilously climbed on a shaky ladder to paint the eaves but I had a little more courage in those days. Mary's father got our garden into shape.

So I settled into the life of a middle-class commuter, leaving home early in the morning to catch the train to London and usually being picked up by Mary in the evening around seven o'clock. We watched the progress of Amanda and Gunter through primary and secondary school, rejoiced at their successes, commiserated at their set-backs, attended parents' evenings, school concerts and fetes, worried when they were late coming home at night. We joined the local Labour Party and I served on its committee for many years. And we went camping in France every year.

I worked at the university for twenty-eight years, the final six years as a part-time consultant. There were many changes over those years. Student numbers increased from the original three thousand to many times that number. The status of engineering declined and that of the social sciences rose. New subjects were introduced: business studies, law, music, nursing, journalism. The old formality went, first names became acceptable as did casual dress.

The many frustrations I experienced at the beginning were

gradually resolved. The public relations office that so irritated me was eventually abolished and I was given sole charge of the University's publicity. I could once again use the leading design studios and printers of my choice. Over the years I produced a vast quantity of printed material, prospectuses, annual reports, brochures, leaflets. All of it was unmemorable, but it needed doing and I think I did it reasonably well.

I came to terms too, with life as a commuter. There was a rhythm to it – sometimes broken. Every week day morning, I set off complete with briefcase, containing a packed lunch of sandwiches, apple and a bun, expandible umbrella, *The Guardian*, book, maybe a few documents from work that I might want to look over just to put my mind at ease. Others would emerge from houses along the route; there would be no greeting, no acknowledgement. But we recognised one another and in an emergency would make contact. If trains were not running because of bad weather or an accident, someone heading home again from the station, to whom I might never otherwise have spoken, would stop and inform me.

Other rituals were observed. At the railway station little groups waited at intervals along the platform close to where there would be a door on the incoming London train. They were seldom far out. Occasionally there would be a rogue train with an unconventional make-up, but there was always someone who could spot this a long way off and then there would be a scramble to take up new positions. I formed a tenuous acquaintanceship with another commuter, a man of around my own age, and for many years we sat together during the morning journey. We would talk about inconsequential matters for about ten minutes and then read our papers for the rest of the journey. We never got to know each other's names or anything about our lives. Nonetheless I think we gave a certain comfort to each other. Some years after I had retired, Mary and I were having a drink in a country pub when he and his wife came in. We had a friendly chat, again about inconsequential matters, and I never saw him after that. I don't think either of us shed any tears.

I was determined not to die of boredom when I retired and in my last year at the University I took up an old occupation of mine and became a bookseller again, this time selling secondhand and antiquarian books. Mary works with me and for over twenty years we have brought out catalogues, concentrating on books about Ireland. Selling books does not have the same cachet as writing them but I suppose it is an honourable enough occupation and has attracted a number of admirable people: George Orwell, Sylvia Beach and that strange Frenchman, whom Geoffrey Hill called "one of the great souls", Charles Peguy.

The years that followed were on the whole happy, but there were sad times. Mary's parents had shown me constant affection from the time I met them. I loved their quirky ways, their generosity, even their artless prejudices. I remember with happiness sunny afternoons seated in their splendid garden enjoying a tea of meat and salad and freshly sliced bread and butter. We would visit, too, Mary's aunts and uncles, all kind hospitable people. But gradually the years would take their toll, an aunt would go and then an uncle. Eventually the health of Mary's parents began to decline. It was a time of great stress, particularly for Mary who would make frequent and often harrowing visits to Heathfield. As their health got worse it was necessary for them to go into a nursing home. Mary's mother, who endured suffering without complaint, was the first to depart. Her father, a strong-willed man, who had developed dementia, did not long survive his wife. They were a fine couple and it was a great privilege to have known them. Like all of us when our parents go, Mary felt regret that she had not done more for them. But I know she did everything she possibly could.

As our children grew up, the summer camping expeditions came to an end. They no longer cared to sit bickering in the back seat of a car without air conditioning, squeezed in by luggage that wouldn't fit in the boot, while being driven for two days at the height of summer through France. I hope like us they will cherish some happy memories of those days.

In the years since we have travelled further afield and in greater comfort and have seen the few things that I suppose a person ought to see during his lifetime, the Taj Mahal and the great palaces and forts of Northern India, St.Petersburg, The Pyramids and the Temples of the Nile, New York, the American West. So life became pretty serene. We had a comfortable home and an acceptable income. We had friends. We went out for meals and up to London to see a play or an exhibition. From time to time we would spend a weekend in Paris or Amsterdam. I was working my way through the nineteenth century novelists and there was much of Trollope still left.

Over the years my ties with Ireland weakened – on the surface at any rate. I had given up membership of The Irish Club some time before our marriage and had lost contact with most of my Irish friends in London. I now lived in a wholly

English milieu with friends who were English and could easily pass for a middle-class Englishman. I have no problems with that. Whatever past sins they may have committed, England and its people have been good to me for half a century and I am grateful to them. Yet I never ceased to feel that I did not totally belong. I could never shed the baggage I had acquired during my first eighteen years. I have remained passionately interested in the fate of Ireland, subscribed to Irish magazines and watched every television programme with an Irish theme, however asinine. I won't change now.

I have kept the faith. It was easier in the fifties and sixties when there was still a cachet attached to being a Catholic.But slowly the situation began to change. It became fashionable for younger people brought up as Catholics – especially those in the public eye - to declare they no longer believed. Seminaries and convents began to close. Battles were fought with the state over abortion and the rights of homosexuals and continue still. Recently there has been the scandal of paedophile priests. We have no more intellectual giants on our side: no successors to Greene and Waugh, no outstanding theologians to cross swords on our behalf with the increasingly militant atheists: I have even very grave doubts as to whether Fathers Knox and Darcy were the brilliant minds I once thought. And there has been a disturbing rise in conservatism within the church, exemplified by an organisation such as Opus Dei. These are not entirely comfortable days for believers with a liberal turn of mind.

As I grew older the desire to make a name in literature, as with other desires, became weaker. I had become aware that literary fame was a fickle commodity. I had known a few writers who achieved some renown in their day and were now practically forgotten. Besides, it is probably not a good idea to think of writing fiction when you have passed a certain age. The reading public is not greatly receptive to the amours of elderly men and women.

And yet, somewhere in the recesses of my mind there still lurked that unextinguishable longing to express my secret feelings, even if only a handful of others would listen. It was how the composer Ernest Chausson felt: "I would not want to go under without having written something, be it no more than a page, that goes to the heart".

I felt guilty that I had squandered so many years in a kind of arrogant refusal to put pen to paper. Not so long before she died, my mother had unexpectedly said to me: "Anthony, weren't you going to write a book once?" I mumbled some sort of non-committal reply but her words struck home. I remembered the story that she had told me about The Poet saying that he knew me – that I was a writer. It had amused her but I think that she had also been proud to think that I might make a career in literature. My father had boasted to his friends about those poor little articles I had written.

At one time I had entertained the romantic thought that I might act as D.H. Lawrence had done with his first novel The White Peacock. When he knew his mother was dying he had asked the publishers to speed up the printing so that she could see it before it was too late. "The very first copy of the White Peacock that was ever sent out, I put in my mother's hands when she lay dying. She looked at the outside, and then at me with darkening eyes". But for me it was not to be.

I had not forgotten John McGahern. I was getting old now

and so too was he, and I thought that perhaps before it was too late I would get in touch with him. The opportunity came in 1992. That was the year his collected short stories were published and I saw in *The Guardian* that he was giving a reading in the Queen Elizabeth Hall on the South Bank around the time of publication. I discussed with Mary whether I should maintain my silence or take the opportunity of renewing our friendship – or at least our acquaintance. Mary thought I should go.

I felt uneasy about it all. I did not know what the drill was for arranging such a meeting. I was nervous about public places. It was, after all, a quarter of a century since I had seen him in those unhappy circumstances. Life had altered greatly for both of us but his life had changed more dramatically than mine. I knew he had won awards and honours and taught at universities in America and France. It was possible that he had long forgotten about me. But I also remembered the early days of our acquaintance, that first meeting in the hostel in Stepney, our meals in our lodgings in Dublin, the walk along the river Boyne and his weekend in my home town, and his eagerness to talk to me about books when he was young.

It was pretty empty in the foyer of the Queen Elizabeth Hall when I got there. A young woman was opening up packages of books. I assumed she was from his publisher, Faber. I asked her if she thought it would be possible for me to have a word with John McGahern after the reading. She told me to speak with a young man who would appear from time to time in a state of some anxiety. I managed to catch hold of him and quickly explained that I was an old friend of John's. Could he take a message to him? He hesitated at first and then reluctantly agreed and said there was no possibility of seeing him before the reading. I scribbled on a piece of paper "John, its Tony Whelan. Would it be possible to see you after the reading?" The young man went off with the note and a few moments later John appeared, a smile on his face, his hand outstretched. "How are you, Tony" he asked. He was smartly dressed in a grey suit and sewn on the lapel of the jacket was the insignia of the Chevalier de L'ordre des Arts et des Lettres which he had been awarded by the government of France. I was touched by this little conceit which I never saw him wear again. He explained he was feeling very nervous about the reading and I wished him luck. He promised to see me afterwards.

Unlike his later readings this one was not well attended. His reputation had not yet seeped through to all those in London and its surroundings who were interested in Irish literature. In the thirty years since the publication of *The Barracks* he had written only four other novels, not many compared to other writers who feel they must produce a new work every other year to keep themselves in the public eye. It would yet be a few more years before John would fill the same hall with a reading from his final novel *That They May Face the Rising Son* and *Memoir*. I had never been to a reading before and was surprised at how short it was. There were questions afterwards which John answered with great consideration. On the whole I am of the opinion that those who ask questions on such occasions are more concerned about having their own views heard and their literary knowledge admired than about learning the views of the speaker. Afterwards there was a signing and when it was over John talked with me for a while and introduced me to the members of his family who were there. He apologised that he was going out for a meal with them but asked me to call and visit him and Madeline when I was next in Ireland. I asked him to sign a copy of the book and he touchingly wrote on the title-page: " For Tony with constant affection. John".

Going home on the train I thought over the experience. I was surprised and pleased that he should have come out to see me just before the talk and I wondered if he had ever thought about me over the past quarter of a century. He did not of course ask me anything about my writing then, nor would he ever in the subsequent years. I knew that we could not have the same easy relationship that we once had. But I was glad that we had met up again.

EIGHT

In the summer of 1993 we paid our first visit to Ireland for several years. The recent past had been a difficult time for Mary. There had been the death of her parents earlier in the year and before that several stressful months during their final illnesses. We decided that a few days in a decent hotel in pleasant surroundings would be a good restorative, and we could think of no more appropriate location that the West Coast of Ireland.

There was one other reason for our visit to Ireland. I was coming to the end of my time at the university and Mary, too, was considering retiring. We had lived in Tonbridge for over twenty years and it had served us well, but life in this area of England had gradually become more frenetic and, like many people in our circumstances, we had from time to time yearned for somewhere with a gentler pace to which we could occasionally escape. We had been careful with our money and had a little surplus to invest in a small property, when we could find the right location.

Some of our friends had bought second homes in France and for us France seemed a pretty obvious choice. It was a short ferry crossing away and it was a country we had visited many times and greatly admired. It had beautiful unspoilt countryside, wonderful cities and towns and we had always found the people friendly and helpful. And, of course, there was the excellent and inexpensive food and wine. For me there were other attachments. However wayward they might be, I would always regard the French as co-religionists. France had the great shrines of Lourdes and Lisieux, wonderful cathedrals and abbeys and in every town and every little village there was a church, however empty and neglected, in which I would feel at home. And I liked the way France could produce quirky people of great talent, perhaps genius, who could take religion very seriously, like Charles Peguy, Georges Bernanos, Francis Poulenc, Robert Bresson.

I could also put forward the Irish connection. During our darkest hours had we not been allies? As every Irish school child knows, at the battle of Fontenoy in 1745 the Irish Brigade had turned the tide for France and in 1798 the Directory had sent over General Humbert and 1000 men to aid the fledgling Irish Republic: it was unfortunate that after some early spectacular successes Humbert was forced to surrender to British forces, to be treated with great courtesy, while the hapless Irish army was given no quarter. But, *c'est la guerre*.

So we gave France a lot of thought. If there was anywhere on the mainland of Europe where we would buy a house, it would be France. But in the end we rejected it. Despite our great affection for the place, we knew we could not be at ease there. We could not enter the French world. It was better to leave it as a place to visit.

There was Ireland. It was my homeland. I understood Ireland or believed I did. Mary was always happy in Ireland. So now we toyed with the idea of buying a place there. Once, years earlier, when we were driving from Rosslare, we had looked at places along the coast south of Dublin, but nothing there appealed to us. Nor was the area round my home town, however beautiful and full of memories for me, really possible. I knew Mary could never cope with the religion and the politics and I, too, would now find those things exasperating. The only area that seemed appropriate was the west coast.

Now that I had again made contact with John McGahern, I felt I should fulfil my promise to call on him and Madeline when we were next in Ireland. We had never visited northwest Ireland, the area that comprises Sligo, Leitrim and Donegal. I knew a little about Sligo from its association with Yeats and I had heard about Donegal from my sister, Jean, who had been to Irish Summer Schools there – it was also the county of Seosamh MacGrianna, the *bete noir* of my grammar school days. But of Leitrim, where John lived, I knew nothing.

We found a hotel in Strandhill, a little resort on the coast near Sligo, and booked a few nights accommodation. I rang John and told him of our arrangements and he invited us to call in on our way and have lunch with them. At Mohill we followed his instructions to leave the main road and head north towards Enniskillen, but after a while we became confused. We stopped at a little shop and asked the woman there if she knew where John McGahern lived. She spoke of John with affection, as if he was an old friend, and came out to show us the way. The final part of the journey involved a lengthy drive along a narrow track until we came to the lake that would figure prominently in his final novel. The stone farmhouse was just around the corner. We were welcomed warmly by John and Madeline, a tall slender American in the Katharine Hepburn mould. While Madeline prepared lunch John showed us around the farm, of which he was obviously proud. We were given an excellent lunch and got through a couple of bottles of a Portuguese white wine favoured by John. We talked about our family and about Leitrim and he told us a bit about his working methods and his lecturing assignments in America and France. But we said very little about a subject that was very dear to him and would once have been to me.

In all honesty I suppose I was a bit diffident about getting involved in a discussion on literature. During our meetings a quarter of a century previously he had already achieved a status, certainly in his home country, on the strength of his first two novels and I was aware of it, and so naturally was he. But I was more at ease then as there was still a chance that I might enter the fold. In the years since a great deal had happened. John was no longer the *enfant terrible* of Irish letters but a cherished representative of the national culture. He had long made his peace with the establishments, both clerical and lay. His work was known and acclaimed throughout the English speaking world and beyond, not so much maybe by readers of middlebrow fashionable novels but certainly by critics and serious readers. His most recent novel, *Amongst Women,* had consolidated his position as one of the outstanding fiction writers of the day. No anthology of Irish literature – indeed of modern literature in English – would seem complete without a contribution by him. He was a famous person and fame leaves its mark. And there was one other barrier. Farming, the second trade he now followed, was alien to me. He knew about animals and the land and the seasons, matters that for me were mysteries.

But if he had changed so had I. I had given up – almost – all hope of being a writer and had settled down to a middle class provincial existence. I had been married happily for many years and had two grown-up children. I had my own enthusiasms – I could not imagine John enjoying life on a French campsite. I read voraciously but in my own way. I no longer bothered with reviews of modern literature or took notice of the views of others.

I was glad to have seen John once again and to have met Madeline. It was good to find him settled among his own people and in the land he loved. What he thought about me I did not know or ever will. For my part I would continue to admire his great talent and to be glad that once we had a close relationship; but now that a breach had been healed I assumed that we might well not meet up again. In the event I was wrong.

We drove on to Strandhill through countryside that was unfamiliar, bleak enough and uncultivated, but without the starkness of Connemara. The hotel was small and comfortable and the meals good and substantial. Strandhill had not too much to offer in the way of entertainment but that was not important given its wonderful location. It was within easy reach of Sligo, then a town slowly beginning to wake up from a long period of stagnation, an unpretentious place with old-fashioned drapers shops and tea-rooms where they still brought you out a cake stand from which you helped yourself. We visited the local attractions, many of them associated with Yeats. He is buried not far away in the graveyard of Drumcliffe church and we duly paid our respects. Maybe the inscription on the headstone is a little pretentious but we can forgive him for that. Despite his somewhat aloof manner, those upper-crust foreign friends, his many forays abroad, he stood by his country and brought honour to it. And, to its credit, Ireland stood by him. It is easy enough to smile, but I am proud that Ireland could send a ship from its little navy to bring back the remains of a poet. What other country would do so?

We visited Lisadell,the home of the Gore-Booths, a singularly unattractive nineteenth century mansion, then in a poor state of repair. But a romantic place through its associations with Yeats, who was a frequent visitor, and with the two Gore-Booth women who had been brought up there: Eva, who became a notable socialist, feminist and minor poet, still with some standing in Ireland which does not lightly discard its writers; and Constance who would forsake her heritage to become a highly self-publicising revolutionary.

Also nearby was Knocknarea, a spectacular isolated hill, on the summit of which was an enormous cairn, said to cover the grave of the legendary Queen Maeve. We climbed it on a sunny day and were rewarded with an astonishing view encompassing the holy mountain, Croagh Patrick, to the South and to the North the mountains of Donegal. We walked around the prehistoric tombs at Carraroe and along the golden sands of the beach at Rosses Point that seemed to go on forever. It had been a wonderful holiday and we had found a spot that we would be happy to return to.

On our last day, I spotted an advertisement on the back page of *The Irish Times* offering cottages for sale in Sligo and Leitrim at prices starting at £4000. When we got home we sent for the list. It had details of thirty or so cottages in varying states of repair and it got us very excited. It seemed a very romantic idea to own a little house somewhere in that magical place we had just discovered. We decided to go back in the following February and this time we stayed in a holiday cottage in Dromahair, a village in County Leitrim about twelve miles inland from Sligo.

Dromahair, which we would come to know well, is a very pretty village, among the prettiest in Ireland, with all the usual amenities that still survive in such places: several pubs, shops, a post office, a hotel, a hairdresser's, a garage which doubles as an undertaker's. The river Bonet crosses the road nearby and looking down from a little hill are the romantic ruins of a sixteenth-century Franciscan friary. It is just within the boundaries of the Yeats' Country and gets a mention in one of the early poems.

The day after we arrived we drove into Sligo on a winding road that follows the shore of the beautiful Lough Gill – the lough that holds the Isle of Innisfree. The agent went through his latest list with us, crossing through those he thought would be unsuitable – leaving a half-dozen or so for us to have a look at. We set off with high hopes but we found that most were in poor condition and the rest had one or more fatal flaws.

It was depressing and it seemed that we could be going back to England empty- handed. Two days before we were due to leave, we were looking casually in the window of another estate agent and saw notices for a couple of cottages that looked interesting and affordable. The agent told us where they were and said we would find the keys above the doors. They were not far from one another in a beautiful rural setting with a mountain range visible from the front door. One was in reasonable condition but we decided it was too small. The interior of the other was in a poor condition and, like many derelict Irish cottages, was cluttered up with decaying furniture.

The bathroom was particularly unpleasant. But there was something about the place that appealed to us, and we went back to look at it a couple of times before we went home. Even with our basic knowledge of buildings, we could see there was a lot to be done and in Dromahair we enquired about local builders and were recommended a reliable man.

When we got back to Tonbridge we spent a long time going over the pros and cons of buying the place. We rang the builder and asked him to have a look at the cottage, and he reported back that he would be happy to do the work and gave us a rough price that we considered reasonable. We thought about it for a little longer and then we rang up the agent and said we were interested. He dismissed our suggestion that there should be a survey with the scornful retort that at that price we wouldn't need a survey. He sent us the contract and we signed it.

In June we went back to Dromahair, taking with us Mary's brother, Oliver, one of those men who know about buildings and at a pinch could have built one himself. It was a depressing experience. It was raining, the garden had overgrown and the cottage now looked very dreary. But we felt we could not back out now. We went over the place with the builder and decided, with the advice of Oliver, the alterations we wanted. The next few months were difficult as every week the builder would ring us to report some new defect. But in the end it was all resolved. We stayed there for the first time in September of that year, when it was just about habitable. There was still plenty of rubble around, but the garden had been cleared and there was a new bathroom. The weather was sunny and we could see the distant mountains. It was incredibly peaceful and we felt very happy.

There are still some defects in the house, nothing too serious, but every time we go over there are a few jobs to be done. But other people who have holiday homes tell us the same story. The one-acre garden is far too large but in these parts it seems to be considered a reasonable size. At first I would spend all day strimming the grass but now a neighbour keeps it under control.

We have made many friends among our new neighbours, particularly Peggy and Martin Dolan, whose farm is across the road, and who have shown us great kindness from the moment we first arrived. It took a little time but I think we have now been accepted as part of the community. It is nice that when we go over people will say to us "Welcome home" and after I go to Mass on that first Sunday, I will get a kiss or hug from my women friends, something that would not happen in Tonbridge. The church is a short walk along the road from us, built at a time when there was a more thriving community. I like going to mass there. The atmosphere is homely. Men will still stand by the porch during the service, as they did when I was young, and people go up for communion in a higgledy-piggledy way.

There is no cultivated land around us. The farms are small and will support only sheep and a few cattle. Many of the fields are totally neglected and overgrown with rushes. But, by way of compensation, the hedgerows will have masses of wild flowers in the Spring and Summer and everywhere there are breathtaking views. Although no sort of cultivator myself these days, I can still get a lift when occasionally I see a few drills of potatoes at the side of a house.

Life is so much simpler here: there are no big decisions to be taken. We can always find something to do. Mary cultivates a little patch at the back of the cottage and fights a constant battle with weeds. I have my own work, sawing up timber for firewood, filling in gaps in the plaster, touching up the paintwork. I like such little tasks.

When we can, we shop in Dromahair; we have friends there now and in recent years it has acquired a good restaurant. But I cannot buy *The Guardian* there and so occasionally we will travel the eight miles to Manorhamilton, a down-at-heel but quirky little town, with some unusual features, including a large sculpture workshop. Our main town is Sligo, which now has art galleries, theatres and shopping malls. In fine weather we can drive to the coast, in particular that part North of Sligo on the way to Donegal. There are many little coves where you can rest and look out over the Atlantic and hardly come across another living soul.

Sometimes we venture across the border to shop in Enniskillen, particularly if we are running low on wine. It is a pleasant town and everyone is very helpful but it is different from the South, and although I consider myself an Ulsterman, I feel a little uncomfortable there. Almost at once I find myself trying to work out who is a Catholic and who isn't. That is something that exasperates Mary.

I find it strange, but also satisfying, that I should own a little house and an acre of land in Ireland. On a good day, and there are plenty, it gives me pleasure to watch from the front door the distant hills, not those of my childhood, but some that are also beautiful, perhaps the same Yeats had seen as a child, and, if I am feeling particularly sentimental, recall that two centuries earlier Humbert and his Frenchmen had passed near this place to engage in a hopeless battle and that, over the years, many thousands had suffered and died for this poor land. I don't think I could ever have a permanent home there: too many years, too many events, too many relationships have intervened. But, at least for part of my life, I am no longer an exile.

Of course, I would meet up with John again. We were now reasonably close neighbours. We did not bother each other too much. We had been back to his house and he and Madeline had been to the cottage a few times. I think they were quite impressed. And we met up at other times and places, in Blakes in Enniskillen, Hardagons in Sligo, and in the hotels in Carrick. Our paths would cross, too, at events in the area. John was a strong supporter of local activities and if there was a local book or film to be launched he would be there. His photograph could frequently be seen in the local paper attending some function, often in the company of the parish priest. Although he professed no longer to believe, he felt the place of religion in the life of the community should be acknowledged. We could converse more freely now, and I liked to sound out his views on contemporary writers which he was not slow to offer. Almost always, I am happy to say, our views coincided but on one occasion we had a heated debate about an Irish-American writer, then extremely popular, whom we disliked and whom he strongly championed. Afterwards I wondered for a while if we might have come to the end of our relationship.

There was one more novel to come. His last, *Amongst Women*, had been published in 1990. The next would come out twelve years later. In his long career as a writer of fiction there were only six novels. He was in no great hurry.

That They May Face the Rising Sun was published in 2002 and established him once and for all as a great writer. We were especially fortunate to have had the experience of living in Co. Leitrim over a number of years. It added to our appreciation of what I think is his finest work. We knew a little of those singular people who inhabit the book and of their ways.

Early in 1999 Rita telephoned to tell me about an important event that would take place in Kilkeel in June. There was to be a reunion for pupils of our old primary school, St. Colmans, which had opened a hundred years earlier. Although the original building had been closed in 1963, when a new modern building was opened, the old school was fondly remembered by several generations of people, most of them now getting on in years. Rita offered to get tickets for the reunion for Mary and myself, but I demurred at first. I did not think I could face all those people whom I had known as a child but, in most cases, had not seen for sixty years. But Mary persuaded me to go and it turned out to be one of the most wonderful experiences of my life.

Rita had also told me that the reunion was being held to coincide with the weekend of Cemetery Sunday, an annual event involving an open-air service in the churchyard during which family members gather around the graves of their departed relatives. Mary was not too keen on this sort of event. It was not really in tune with the English psyche. I had never been to one and did not know what to expect.

We booked a room at the local hotel which, as a boy, had

seemed to me a very grand place. When we reached Kilkeel on Saturday afternoon we met up with Rita and Jean and some old friends and arranged to go out for a meal that evening to a restaurant in Annalong, a village a few miles along the coast. Then we walked up to the new school to see an exhibition about its predecessor. There were only a few people in there but among them I recognised an old classmate, who greeted me quite casually as if I had seen him the previous day instead of a great many years ago. Unlike me he had never left the place and was living in happy retirement in the neighbourhood. He had brought along his notebooks about scouting activities,which included several drawings made by me in those distant days. One of the drawings was on display in the exhibition and another was printed in the souvenir programme. I had no recollection of them. Later I came across another old classmate who was looking at my drawings. Gerry had been in the class below me. He too had stayed behind and worked as a fisherman. "You were a great drawer, Tony": he said to me. To tell the truth, I had forgotten about my talent at art. Today, I expect I would have been given a chance to study the subject but there was no hope then.

Mary and I walked down to the beach afterwards and found it in a sorry state with rubbish strewn about liberally and not a sinner around. I thought wistfully of all those summer days I had spent there with my friends, braving the water and lying down afterwards on our skimpy cheap towels, talking about our foolish dreams.

That evening on the way to the restaurant we became involved in that abiding feature of Northern Irish life, a band parade. It was getting towards the twelfth of July and normally there would have been parades of local bands warming up for the big occasion. But this one was on a much bigger scale. The agitation over Drumcree was at its height at the time, and this parade was meant to be a show of strength in support of the Drumcree Orangemen. It was a massive affair with the local bands augmented by a number of militant bands from Belfast. The streets were lined with RUC men and we had to creep along in the car. It made Mary very indignant that we should be intimidated in this way. I noticed in front of one of the Belfast bands a girl carrying the Ulster flag, blonde, attractive, wearing black battle dress, her face fixed with a look of steel. She would have died for her cause and I could not help admiring her.

We had an early breakfast the following morning and went to mass in a small church out in the country. I had not been there since I was a child. As we entered we noticed immediately the stained glass in the window above the altar. Beyond doubt it was the work of Harry Clarke. The builders of medieval cathedrals understood the importance of stained glass as an instrument for worship and so did the wise priest who, sometime in the 1920s, employed the firm of J.S.Clarke and Son to supply this window. There was an excellent choir and a good sermon. At the end we went up and had a closer look at the window. The priest came out and spoke to us and confirmed that it was indeed Harry Clarke's work. Every time we have been back, we have made a point of going to this church.

We drove on and had a look at the cottage, silent and solitary still. It would be a few years before the intrusive new houses would be built. Then we headed up into the mountains and to the Silent Valley, now a vast park with the great dam as centre-piece. The air was so sweet and fresh and it was very peaceful. We had lunch in the hotel with my sisters and our friends. People came over from other tables and talked to us.

The ceremony in the churchyard began at three but we were advised to get there an hour earlier if we wanted to park nearby. There was an enormous crowd in the churchyard of all ages, those old like me, children, young women dressed as if going out for the evening. We stood at our grave with its small neat headstone of Mourne granite. There were just two words: "Whelan, Collins". My mother who had it installed, might well have wanted a more elaborate inscription but she probably feared my criticism. I recognised some of the people at nearby graves and went over and spoke with them. One group comprised a number of brothers who had once lived at the end of the street. It was in their father's shop that my mother had bought the furniture when we moved into the town.

It was a simple enough ceremony. One of the priests came round with holy water and blessed the graves. The rosary was recited. Mary enquired why this happened at such great speed, an awkward question and difficult to answer satisfactorily. There was a sermon and then benediction. It was ages since I had been to benediction. The choir sang those beautiful Latin hymns *Tantum Ergo* and *O Salutaris Hostia*. It was a sunny afternoon and I was standing with my own people by the grave of my parents and my grandparents, who had loved me and to whom I now felt very close. It was impossible for me not to be deeply moved. At such times and in such company you forget the clever people who can put forward such plausible arguments to shake your faith.

In succeeding years we have come back to attend this

ceremony and to see again those childhood friends standing around the family graves.

The main event of the reunion was the social evening, which was held in the assembly hall of the new school. It was crowded by the time we got there. People would come up to me and say "Hello, Anthony", as I was always styled when I was young. Some I would instantly recognise but for others, embarrassingly, I needed prompting. I was embraced affectionately by a nun whom I had not seen since she was a teenage girl. I was really touched that so many people remembered me and, what was even better, remembered me with affection. I moved about in a dreamlike sort of way feeling for the first time in many, many years that I was among people with whom I belonged. I was not an outsider as I had felt at many gatherings. It was a beautiful sensation.

There was a rumour that – incredibly - one of the teachers who had taught me when I was a boy was coming to the event. This was the man who played football with us at lunchtime and who had used his cane on me from time to time. He did indeed turn up, sun-tanned and smartly suited, like an aged film star. I went over and spoke to him and he clasped my hands warmly. He could not recall me but then I would never have known him either. The school put on a little entertainment for us with songs and dances from children who seemed remarkably uninhibited and at ease in their now prosperous world, unlike so many of those I had known long ago, barefooted, pinched, with hard lives ahead for them.

It was sad when it finished, yet I felt very elated as we walked back to the hotel. It was an experience that would never come again. I was so fortunate not to have missed it.

John sounded very casual when he told me of his illness and of the likelihood that he would not recover from it. It was difficult to know how to respond other than murmuring some banality. But even if I had been able to say something immeasurably wise and comforting I don't think he would have needed it. He was in charge of his life and still had one important task to do. I don't know when he began writing *Memoir*, but certainly he timed it well.

Memoir was published in late 2005 and as usual he came over to London to give a reading on the South Bank. The book had been well publicised in advance with extracts in the national papers, and the hall was crowded. We noticed Madeline was in the audience which surprised us as she had not come for his previous readings. John looked well when he came on the stage and he gave his audience a lively performance. Afterwards in the foyer there was a large queue for the book-signing. Before we left we had a brief word with both of them and arranged to meet in Leitrim the following month.

In November we met them in The Bush Hotel in Carrick-on-Shannon. John arrived as usual wearing his belted raincoat and countryman's flat cap. There was a wedding party but we managed to get a seat in a corner of the bar. They were both in good spirits. I suppose I should have remembered all of what was said, but what I remember was trivial: his dislike of the large new supermarket that had just opened in the town and his surprise at the cost of an orange juice. We saw them as far as the car park. That was the last time I saw him.

We were in Ireland the following March. Nearly always when

we are over we spend a day in Galway, taking with us two women friends who live nearby. I go my own way in Galway and we had arranged to meet up later. I was looking through the magazines in Easons when Mary came rushing in. She told me she had just had a phone call from our friend Inga in Dromahair to say it had been announced on the radio that John McGahern had died in hospital in Dublin.

This news hit me badly. I did something very cliched. I went into the nearby St.Nicholas Church. It is a Protestant church, pristine inside and free from the distracting clutter of our own churches. I just sat down there in the quiet and prayed. He had told me a number of times that he did not believe any more, but that didn't matter. He would know the truth of it now.

When we met up again I told Mary we would have to find out the time and place of the funeral. And I suppose in her English way she asked me if I thought we ought to go – that maybe they did not want strangers. I told her I did not consider myself a stranger, that I had once been a friend and maybe always had been one.

On the Saturday morning we made the journey to the little hamlet of Aughawillan where the burial service would take place and where John's mother had been buried. Cars were already parked all along the roads leading to the church and we had to leave ours some distance away. The church was packed but we were able to squeeze in at the back. There was much cameraderie among our group. I was found a seat. The old man beside me told me with pride that the celebrating priest was his nephew. We watched some of the special guests arrive: poet and Nobel Laureate Seamus Heaney and the playwright Brian Friel, a government minister and army officers representing the President and the Taoiseach.

The journey of the cortege from Dublin was reported in *The Leitrim Observer*:

> "As John's remains wound their way from Dublin to Aughawillan they passed through most towns and villages anonymously but when they reached the borders of Co. Leitrim the local people came forward to pay their respects. In Dromod, Mohill, Fenagh and Ballinamore crowds of people, many strangers, lined the road in silent tribute.
>
> The silence continued as John's remains arrived in Aughnawillan and were carried into the church. No music to distract the emotions of those gathered, just a quiet procession of priests and family following the coffin".

John had arranged his funeral service with a close friend and relation, Father Liam Kelly. It was a simple requiem mass with no hymns or music, something after my own heart. In addition to Father Kelly there were seven other priests taking part in the ceremony. Not bad for a supposed non-believer. Father Kelly preached a good sermon quoting Marcel Proust, probably for the first time in a Catholic church in Ireland. Then they carried out the coffin, followed by Madeline, a proud figure. He was buried beside his mother, and, in accordance with Irish custom and at his own request, a decade of the rosary was recited. The sun had been shining earlier but now a light rain began to fall as if to remind us that we were in Leitrim. Afterwards and again in accordance with Irish custom there was a splendid lunch in the Landmark Hotel in Carrick-on-Shannon. I found myself seated beside his editor at Faber, who had been taught by him as a young boy. As we said goodbye to Madeline she thanked us for coming but I was glad to have been there.

I have thought since of those forlorn words he wrote to me long ago "I still teach in Dublin. I often fear I shall grow old among the primers and children who care as little about learning as I do about teaching". I have kept that letter. Perhaps I had sensed that that would not be his fate.

It had been in my mind to write this for some time and I started working on it in earnest soon after I returned from the funeral. Maybe I had waited so I could include my memories of John without too much fear of contradiction. I hope I have said nothing that could offend him. If it has any virtue, it will be because I have tried to follow the standards he had always observed.

I am now eighty-two and that is hard to accept. I have always thought of myself as being young with a future still stretching ahead. I don't suppose that feeling will change. Although there have been difficult moments in my life I am not unhappy with the cards that have been dealt to me. I had the good fortune to have been born in Ireland and into the Catholic Faith: to both I have retained an allegiance that has often been faltering and ambiguous. I was given loving parents and two dear sisters who have always remained close to me. At a time when my future seemed bleak, Mary came into my life and over many years has given a love that I have not deserved. Together we had the privilege of bringing up a daughter and a son who have now found their own places in the world. We have beautiful and good grandchildren. And many kind friends and relatives. We have acquired a new home in Ireland. My adopted country has treated me with tolerance and generosity: I regret that I cannot share all its enthusiasms but I can understand, I think, and accept them.

I did not fulfil my ambition to become a writer. It does not matter. Even if I had persevered, the results would never have been more than mediocre and there are plenty of mediocre writers already. I'll leave it at that.